GRANDCHILDREN OF ALCOHOLICS

Another Generation of Co-dependency

Ann W. Smith

 Health Communications, Inc.
Deerfield Beach, Florida

Ann W. Smith
The Caron Foundation
Wernersville, Pennsylvania

Library of Congress Cataloging-in-Publication Data
Smith, Ann (Ann W.), 1950-
    Grandchildren of Alcoholics.

    1. Grandchildren of alcoholics--United States.
I. Title.
HV5132.S65   1988   362.2'92   87-23594
ISBN 0932194-55-9

©1988 Ann W. Smith
ISBN 0-932194-55-9

Cover design by Reta Kaufman

Published by Health Communications, Inc.
        Enterprise Center
        3201 SW 15th Street
        Deerfield Beach, FL 33442

Acknowledgments

My thanks to the special people who made this book a reality:

Rick Esterly and Sharon Wegscheider-Cruse, two very special mentors who believed in what I had to say and gave me the push to begin to write it down.

The staff of the Caron Foundation Family Program, for their inspiration and support.

The grandchildren of alcoholics who have encouraged me to speak for them, especially those interviewed.

The U.S. Journal staff, especially Peter Vegso and Gary Seidler.

My children, Jeff and Lindsay, who give me joy and hope.

Contents

Introduction

I have always believed that there is more to chemical dependency than just the effects on the consumer of the chemical. This belief has been based on growing up in a family where, with the exception of my own parents, alcoholism is a common occurrence. In my 14 years of working with chemically dependent persons and their families it has become increasingly clear that once the chemical has been removed and the brief period of relief exhausted, there remains a family system that has become very skilled at adapting to dysfunction and has no tools with which to cope with a lack of crises. Therefore, a crisis is quickly recreated with new addictions or compulsions, physical and/or emotional illness or even relapse in an effort to maintain the status quo.

My work in an intensive treatment program for Adult Children of Alcoholics and my teaching about co-dependency have introduced me to many individuals whose present lives are strikingly similar to ACoAs but who have not been able to identify the dysfunction or any obvious symptom in their family of origin. This group very often is made up of Grandchildren of Alcoholics (GCoAs), many of whom have never been told and do not know that there was addiction in a grandparent or even several grandparents.

They do not feel justified in their pain and current life problems and therefore do not seek help. A few have fortunately been exposed to ACoA self-help and treatment through their own recovery in Alcoholics Anonymous. However they report feeling out of place without a real "story" to tell. Many GCoAs question "How did I get this messed up in such a good family?"

My concern for this as yet unidentified group of hurting people is the motivation behind this book. In addition, it would be dishonest not to acknowledge my hope for personal validation through the study of the experiences of other Grandchildren of Alcoholics.

My personal search and, more recently, my contacts with other Grandchildren have made me aware of our strong fear of disloyalty to our parents who were so invested in trying to make it different for us. On behalf of all GCoAs, I want to recognize that effort and express our appreciation for the obstacles they, our parents, had to overcome as Adult Children of Alcoholics to raise us the best way they knew how. Admitting that it could have been better does not negate the efforts that were made. The proof of the existence of co-dependency in our families is shown in the lives of GCoAs, who, like their ACoA counterparts, are in varying degrees of dysfunction in their adult lives.

My goals in writing this book are numerous. However my primary aim is to serve as an advocate for Grandchildren, giving them the validation that, *Yes, there was something wrong. No, it is not your fault*, and, *Yes, it is okay to talk about it.*

My apologies for introducing another "label". I know of no other way to bring this group of people out of hiding and into recovery.

_____ Chapter 1 _____

CO-DEPENDENCY: A Multigenerational View

When I reflect on the changes that have occurred in our perceptions of chemical dependency and its effect on the family since the early years in the treatment field, I am overwhelmed with how fast and far we have come. I'm sure many professionals, myself included, would like to attribute this solely to our genius and expertise, however most will admit that what we do know, we have learned from our clients and/or our own personal growth. Our willingness to listen, observe and change with our clients is one of the things that makes us special.

It was not that long ago when the phrase "Who wouldn't drink with a wife like that?" was representative of the prevailing belief regarding the family of the alcoholic. The time period itself depends upon what part of the country we are in, and in some areas, these attitudes may still exist. At that time, treatment programs were designed to insulate the chemically dependent person from those "crazy people" at home, and other than an occasional referral to Al-Anon, no effort was made to address family issues.

As we became more knowledgeable of the recovery process for the alcoholic, we were conscious that it was advantageous to teach the family to support the newly recovered person in maintaining sobriety, i.e., be supportive of AA attendance, don't bring up the past, be patient, etc. Through efforts to educate the family and prevent the sabotaging of the alcoholic's recovery, we began to spend more time with spouses. They, themselves, began to teach us about what we now call co-dependency.

This initial contact with spouses was for me, and I suspect for many other professionals, the beginning of a dramatic change in the way I viewed the disease of alcoholism. Our previous simplistic belief that once the chemical is removed, it would just be a matter of time before things improved at home, began to dissolve. The question of why someone would stay in an abusive marriage with no apparent payoff, the panic that appeared in the spouse when the alcoholic got sober, the extreme low self-worth, depression, total addiction to another person, could not be explained that easily. Upon closer examination, the fact that most spouses came from either alcoholic or dysfunctional families themselves provided a more plausible explanation.

The term "co-dependency" within the addiction field applies to spouses or any intimate partner, children and adult children of alcoholics. More recently it has included the chemically dependent person who has obviously lived around the dynamics of the same family system. A broader view would encompass anyone living in a dysfunctional family system, which encourages dependent relationships. The original term co-dependent reflected the belief that family members became sick along with (Co) the chemically dependent person.

My personal definition of co-dependency is that it is a condition, actually a state of being, that results from adapting to dysfunction (possibly addiction) in a significant other. It is a learned response to stress, which over a person's lifetime can become a way of being, rather than an appropriate means of survival. It is most evident when the co-dependent is removed from the stressor and they respond to their environment as if the threat of harm were still there.

In families where there is physical or even verbal abuse, it is necessary to develop rules for conduct to protect oneself from assault. This is a very sensible thing to do. One such rule might be — don't express anger or disagree or someone will get hurt. Other seemingly dysfunctional rules like, don't trust, don't be vulnerable or get close, don't touch, may also be born of necessity and be very functional rules in a particular family system.

These rules however do not prepare us for the world of intimacy and healthy relating. Unfortunately, those who are born into a system where survival rules are necessary, are not aware, nor are they told, that these rules don't apply to life outside of this family. The obvious result is that the patterns continue. Co-dependents find other co-dependents to relate to, and live in a constant state of crisis, either internally or externally. They are not choosing to be in dysfunctional relationships, they are just naturally attracted to and by other chemically dependent and co-dependent people. In this way, through family rules, belief systems and behavior patterns, co-dependency is passed on to further generations, even when the chemical dependency is not.

Many of us have heard others ask the question "Why do I identify with Adult Children of Alcoholics when my parents didn't drink?" The answer lies not in the family's addiction or lack of it, but in the co-dependent family dynamics which are subtly passed on from one generation to the next.

It is interesting that even in families where chemical dependency is openly acknowledged, there remains total denial of the effect this may have had on the family. The following quote from a grandchild of an alcoholic shows this quite clearly:

"My maternal Grandfather was alcoholic and when drunk would threaten his children with a gun and dare them to get off the sofa. I never knew him. He died when my mother was 15. My father came home drunk once when I was a baby and my mother said she would not have her children growing up around a drunk. To my knowledge Dad never abused alcohol after that. Our family problems did not seem to be related to alcoholism." Adult children of alcoholics, being the survivors that they are, find ways to overcome unimaginable abuses and hurts as children. Each wants to believe he/she can overcome these horrors of childhood. They attempt to control the uncontrollable, in this case, even prevent alcoholism. They must work very hard to convince themselves that the past is behind them and will not affect their children, even convincing their children there is nothing wrong.

This denial is reflected frequently in the belief that we must be around the actual drinking or chemical use in order to be affected by it. Many families, where alcoholism is present, have lived through periods of sobriety where the stress actually increased with the abstinence. Divorce, separation, even the death of the drinking person, does not remove the co-dependent dynamics from the family system. Without the identifiable stressor to explain the dysfunction of the family system, the problem goes underground. It is no longer discussed or focused on outwardly. Other scapegoats or problems may be found, but it lives on and will undoubtedly return in the lives of the children or grandchildren.

Consquences For Adult Children of Alcoholics

Not all children of alcoholics are affected by the disease in the same way. As Robert Ackerman states in his book, *Children Of Alcoholics,* it may depend on the degree (i.e., severity), the type of alcoholic parent and the individual perception of the child. We cannot assume that all ACoAs share all of the same characteristics. I do believe we can assume that being raised in an alcoholic or chemically dependent home leaves the majority of ACoAs handicapped in some fairly predictable ways, and without some form of treatment, will affect their parenting of their own children later on.

*Low Self-worth

It is impossible to live in an environment of emotional neglect and, at best, inconsistent nurturing and come out feeling good about yourself. The evidence of low self-worth in the ACoA depends somewhat on their role in the family.

The family Hero (Wegscheider-Cruse, *Another Chance*), may be the most difficult to recognize as a victim of low self-worth due to his tendency to look good on the outside. Catch this person on a bad day, however, when he or she has made a mistake, missed a deadline, disappointed a friend or said an unkind word, and you will see the deep-rooted sense of inadequacy. The hero's constant efforts to please and earn the approval of others, particularly family, are motivated by a very poor self-concept. They and other ACoAs love themselves conditionally, which is to say "I am okay if . . .". They wait for the day when they have "it" all together to begin to appreciate their many accomplishments.

Scapegoats exhibit low self-worth in their outwardly self-destructive behaviors. This is carried into adult life in the form of resistance to authority, defiance and at times uncontrollable temper or even rage. Often scapegoats become abusive to others, acting out the internal conflict and self-hate. Despite their determination to be different, they may become very much like the alcoholic parent they hate.

The Lost Child suffers from persistent feelings of inadequacy, feeling less than others, lost and alone in a world they don't understand, in fact, are terrified of. They wear their low self-worth both inside and out, often appearing extremely shy and withdrawn. Like the hero, lost children may be quite talented and creative, but cannot enjoy their successes or share them with others. **The Family Mascot** seeks constant attention through humor, fragility, illness, etc., which is his or her way of saying "I hurt". Like the scapegoat, this may evoke negative responses from the family so instead of easing the pain and inadequacy, it reinforces it.

Many Adult Children believe that since they do not remember the active drinking, did not witness it personally or were "too young", they should not feel badly about themselves. But child psychologists agree that the first five years of life are crucial to the formation of a healthy and positive concept of self. Much of the damage can occur before the memory of the child. ACoAs are adept at changing their outsides to convince the world that they are okay, hoping to convince themselves in the process. Improving self-worth is not accomplished from the outside in, however. This leads to the "imposter syndrome", constant fear of being found out for who they really are. Fortunately, as the efforts to compensate for low self-worth continue, they may become very competent, even successful people. In recovery they will learn not to discount what they are good at and to accept their assets and liabilities equally.

*External Focus

Chemically dependent families foster the idea that if we wait long enough, things will improve without any deliberate action. Living constantly in a stressful environment where feelings of helplessness prevail, leads to the belief that there is no use in trying to change things because it won't do any good. This is often the result of putting a great deal of energy into addressing the wrong problems in the first place. Rarely do family members know exactly what is wrong, and even when they do, they may encounter relatives or professionals who further frustrate their efforts by telling them to be more patient or to get out entirely. They gradually become passive victims to the inevitable progression of the disease, waiting for the spontaneous insight which does not come. Children of alcoholics have many years experience watching the non-alcoholic parent adapt to the insanity in this helpless pattern. Even though children may believe something could have been done, and may even be furious at their parent, the model of passivity stays imbedded in their minds and will be apparent in the manner in which they address life's problems as adults.

ACoAs see themselves as victims of circumstance, unable to exercise any control over the events in their lives. They may, for example, view marriage as something that just works itself out if the right people are together. The solutions to problems in relationships lie with the other person's willingness to change. They are unable to see that their own reactions to problems may be worsening a stressful situation. They believe they have no control over their thoughts or feelings and thus must react automatically with anger, guilt or fear whenever others "provoke" them. The phrase, "He knows how to push my buttons" is a familiar one, suggesting that we have no power over our own reactions to others.

When an ACoA gets up in the morning, he judges the

quality of the day ahead based on what others are doing, thinking, feeling and how "things" are going. They have often been called "hypervigilant" because of their extreme interest in, and ability to pick up on external cues, e.g., facial expressions, the mood of a room, etc. This skill is developed out of necessity in the alcoholic family, where the family mood totally depends upon what the alcoholic is doing today or did last night.

The external focus of a chemically dependent family leads the ACoA to live in reaction to the world, often holding others responsible for the way they feel or even decisions they make. An absence of choice in jobs, relationships, health matters, etc. leads to repressed anger and a set-up for continued victimization. They are sincerely deluded, and believe that when "things" change, they will be okay.

*Unable to Identify or Express Feelings

Expecting an Adult Child to be able to express feelings would be like expecting all Americans to speak Russian without ever having heard it. Although most of us are aware at some level of our physiological responses to our feelings, learning to label those feelings and express them appropriately is something that requires a degree of training or modeling, normally provided in the family environment. When this modeling is not available or may even be violent or otherwise damaging, children have several alternatives. Although none are chosen consciously, there seem to be patterns that emerge.

One pattern is the ACoA who thinks about feelings and may learn to "fit" in by imitating the responses and behavior of others. They become acutely aware of how they should feel and may even know how to act out this feeling, but may not actually "feel" anything in the active sense of the word. Eventually they shut down and lose touch with their own insides, possibly even losing the physiological responses which occur spontaneously for others. Their affect and expression may become mono- tone and numb. An example often given is that of an inability to experience grief at the loss of a loved one. The ACoA who is shut down may be expert at taking care of others who are in pain, but cannot seem to get in touch with his/her own losses.

Some ACoAs give themselves permission to feel certain feelings, for example anger, but not others, vulnerability, sadness, etc. Family scapegoats often look like very angry individuals, but in treatment we discover that for them, anger has become a defense, rather than a feeling. When they are hurt, afraid or sad, they respond with aggressive outbursts. Not only are they using this response to cover pain and keep others at a distance, it may be a pattern which was modeled for the individual by an alcoholic parent and therefore operates instinc- tively without any thought or choice involved.

Women may fear anger and permit themselves to cry openly but never express anger. Adult children who have lived with inappropriate expression of anger, or no expression at all, are left with a terror of anger, assuming that all anger is rage. They believe that if they begin to express it, they will lose all control and either self- destruct or severely hurt others. They may see rage as a normal reaction to a broken shoelace, rather than an extreme response to tragedy like rape, robbery or abuse.

Regardless of the pattern, the inability to identify and express feelings leads to frustrated attempts at intimacy. If you know how I feel, you know me. If I don't know how I feel, and even if I did, couldn't tell you, we will never be able to connect in an intimate way. Adult children are most comfortable with others who have the same or similar level of ability to feel. The obvious outcome is the marriage of two "half persons" trying to make a whole.

*Cannot Ask For Help

The rules in a chemically dependent or severely stressed family are designed to protect the individuals and the system from further trauma. Ironically, it is often assumed that if outsiders knew about the problem, no matter how trivial or serious, it would only make things worse. A sad fact is that in many cases this belief is based on reality. We are all aware of the impact of misinformed professionals and family members attempting to address alcoholism and instead prolonging the problem.

Since denial is the major symptom of alcoholism, it is the nature of the illness to cover up the drinking or chemical use, as well as the resulting family difficulties. It is also believed that if we don't acknowledge the problems, they may go away.

The self-esteem of children of alcoholics is very much dependent on the way others view them. It may also depend on the opinions, approval or disapproval of their families. It is very natural for children to be proud of their parents and siblings, however, when they sense that this family is somehow different from others, they begin to protect the family system (for their own self-esteem and that of the family) from the disapproval of the world. Thus secrets and half-truths become a way of survival. Added to this might be the fear of an angry parent or parents should the truth be exposed.

Keeping the "big secret" whether addiction, incest, abuse, etc., is more important than the needs of the child to talk about his/her feelings. There is an underlying belief that if it is not said out loud, it doesn't exist. Siblings may together witness traumatic incidents of violence and will most likely never discuss it, even privately. Repression permits individuals to block out, or forget, painful experiences.

It is a fact of life in a chemically dependent family that if you don't take care of yourself, no one else will. It is also obvious to children that neither parent has energy, emotional or physical, to spare. Whether out of necessity, fear of trusting or just defiance, children of alcoholics learn to care for themselves. Their efforts to do so are appreciated, maybe even rewarded by the family system, ("At least we don't have to worry about Jane") and thus reinforced. As with any pattern of behavior, the earlier it begins, the less consciously it is performed and the more likely it is to become a way of life.

As adults, children of alcoholics stop expecting others to want to help and become unable to ask for the simplest of things from others, like a ride to work or a cup of coffee. At the same time they may become compulsive about helping others, even when it is not necessary or deserved.

This pattern of avoidance of identifying, talking about and getting help for personal difficulties leads to the exacerbation of those problems and the need for further denial. It does not seem to matter whether the problems are major and minor, the reaction in adult children of alcoholics is the same.

*Extreme Thinking

Our ability to make decisions, look at alternatives and act appropriately in difficult situations depends a great deal on the example set for us in our family of origin. Alcoholic families, obviously stressed, have unique ways of coping with the stress of addiction as well as the everyday problems which arise in any family. The most common immediate response to crises in these families is "This isn't happening", which tends to postpone the problem until it gets a little worse and cannot be avoided. Many times individuals are forced to face growing difficulties because of outside pressure, e.g., school authorities, bill collectors, etc.

For example, a common stressor in alcoholic families

is that of a teenager abusing drugs. In healthy families parents and siblings would be aware of the gradual deterioration of the child. When parental alcoholism is present, teen drug abuse is ignored until the child is in serious legal or health trouble and the authorities intervene and force action. Extreme thinking leads family members to either do nothing or do something crazy.

When a situation must be confronted, the process of decision-making and taking action may be one of blaming, and then drastic or very passive responses.

One ACoA shared, "When we had a problem in our family, the first thing my dad would do was find out whose fault it was. Even if it upset the whole house, he had to blame someone and scream for a while. Nothing was ever talked through or resolved."

Parents may use aggressive threats as a desperate attempt to demonstrate authority, and instead show the panic and fear which prevail on a daily basis. Lack of follow-through on threats tells the children once more that nothing will change. Fear of expressing opinions and feelings prevents family members from thoroughly discussing and negotiating for change. Silence becomes a communicator of disapproval and anger. The dominant person may use power, even violence, to restore order and once again, the problem goes underground only to resurface at a later date.

This is the modeling which children of alcoholics witness and with this minimal preparation for adult life, they repeat these patterns in their relationships, in the workplace and eventually in their parenting.

Adult Children of Alcoholics As Parents

Although low self-worth, external focus, inability to identify or express feelings, inability to ask for help, and extreme thinking are by no means an exhaustive list, they serve as a framework with which to examine the difficulties ACoAs will experience in trying to be effective parents themselves.

ACoAs with low self-worth approach parenthood with an underlying agenda of creating the family they always wished they had as children. The assumption is that they will feel better about themselves if this is accomplished. They may decide to be different from one or both of their parents. Unless they themselves become chemically dependent or severely dysfunctional in some other way, they may partially accomplish these goals.

Claudia Black's book *It Will Never Happen To Me* is the motto of children coming out of alcoholic homes and represents their determination to do it differently. Unfortunately despite their strong motivation to change family patterns and break the addiction cycle, they have only the images and fantasies of television characters, books they have read or perhaps the seemingly happy homes of neighbors or friends from which to draw information.

In the past "Ozzie and Harriet", "Donna Reed", "Father Knows Best" represented the "healthy" people who knew how to do it right. Unfortunately, no one ever noticed that Ozzie never went to work and Adult Children were led to believe that there were perfect families out there who were relatively stress-free. If only they tried hard enough, they could figure out how to do it. Using their intelligence and ability to survive, many ACoAs were able to change the external appearances of their new families so that they did not resemble that of the ones they grew up in. No one drank, yelled, hit or threatened to leave.

As long as they are in an area requiring an external adjustment, ACoAs are successful, but the one variable they are not able to control is their own inside reaction to their children and spouse.

Virginia Satir in *Conjoint Family Therapy* states:

"If the mates have low self-esteem and little trust in each other, they will expect their child to enhance their self-esteem, to be an extension of themselves and to serve crucial pain-relieving functions in the marital relationship."

The manifestation of the ACoAs' low self-worth appears in the emotional interactions between parents, and parent to child. The investment in making this family different from their family of origin is a powerful force which requires total family participation. Often there is excessive consciousness of the image projected to those outside the family.

The message given is "We are a good family" and children (the Grandchildren of Alcoholics) are expected to carry this message to the community through their behavior, appearances and achievements. If children do this well, the self-worth of the parents is enhanced and they have succeeded in overcoming the past, at least temporarily. If they fail, and do not meet the expectations of the ACoA parent, both the parent and child lose self-worth. The child feels an extremely heavy burden internally but is not able to connect this to the low self-worth of the parent. Instead they perceive this as positive interest on the part of the ACoA parent and are grateful for the attention to their activities.

Double Messages

The communication of this conflict to the GCoA is very subtle in the form of excessive expectations and over-concern for the well-being and success of children. Double messages are given since the ACoA parent knows what he/she should say but is unable to live the message or rule himself.

Examples of confusing messages are:
"Be yourself — but do it the right way",
"You are very, very, very important to me",
"I care how you feel, but I'll fall apart if you tell me",
"I know you don't have any problems, but if you ever do, feel free to come to me".

ACoA parents try very hard to show their love by doing the "right" things and assume that their children will feel the love through the "things" that are done for them. What is obviously lacking is the ability to be intimate, and to actually love freely and openly, expressing this love unconditionally both in words and in outward affection. ACoAs with low self-worth fear the rejection and possible abandonment by their children (or anyone else) and remain well defended, even in their parental role.

The external focus of the ACoA leads to parenting with a "Do as I say, but I can't do it myself" model. ACoA parents may make very affirming statements to their children.

For example: "You deserve a good life. Feelings are okay. You should never allow anyone to abuse you. You can be anything you want to be."

Their behavior, however, may say something entirely different. Without the necessary self-esteem, they continue to live as victims of circumstance — too old, too poor, too uneducated, too locked in to make any of the changes they recommend to their children. Frequently their marriages, although externally stable, are spiritually dead, lacking the affection, intimacy and communication they want their children to have. Some may even be abusive or at least neglectful in their relationships. Despite the way they are living, they desperately want their children to do it otherwise. What they model, however, is much more important than what they say. The model is one of waiting for problems to go away, waiting for others to change, waiting for the right set of circumstances to correct the situation, using expressions like "after Christmas . . . when Dad gets a new job . . . in the summer . . . after graduation . . . when we have more money . . ."

Vacations, holidays, and any special event may be expected to make everyone happy and even solve serious marital or other relationship problems. The disappointment that naturally occurs is quickly forgotten in favor of focusing on the next potential "fix".

In their determination to overcome the pains and hurts of their own childhood, ACoAs learn the language of a healthy family (with the exception of the feeling language) and learn how to show the external appearance of a functional family system, without really living it out themselves. The result is an obviously sincere but futile effort to convince themselves and their children (the Grandchildren of Alcoholics) that they are okay.

Volumes could be written about the impact of an inability to identify and express feelings on the family system. ACoAs enter into relationships with the belief that they can create intimacy in their marriages and in their parent/child relationships by simply resolving to do so. However, since they are unable to experience their own feelings and express them openly or appropriately, they cannot model or teach their children. They have a sense of how things ought to be and may even verbalize to their children that they ought to express their feelings, but without the ability to demonstrate this skill to their children, the verbal permission is not taken seriously.

The ACoA parent may say "I want to know how you feel" but then pulls away, changes the subject, gives advice or possibly over-reacts to the child when he or she is open about feelings. Children are naturally protective of the feelings of parents and sensing the discomfort or emotional pain of the ACoA parent, the child will learn to express only what is well received by the parent.

For example, if every time a child expresses his hurt feelings to his mother, she looks worried, he won't feel comfortable telling her again. This reaction by a child is unconscious and rarely verbalized.

The ACoAs Inability to Model Appropriate Emotions Through Parenting

The ACoA's desire to be emotionally available and expressive within family relationships may be sensed by the child when the parent sincerely tries to connect. The effort, however, is thwarted by their own recurring fear of rejection and/or abandonment. Instead of expressing the fear openly, the ACoA uses familiar survival skills, once useful in an active alcoholic family, like withdrawal, silence or angry outbursts. Compulsive behaviors such as working, cleaning and caretaking may serve as seemingly healthy ways to repress pain.

In an effort to bring joy to the family, the ACoA parent may use outside family activities to create fun and enjoyment. Generally, ACoAs have not been exposed to healthy fun and family togetherness as children, and may take even a positive activity to the extreme. "This is good for you. You *will* enjoy it" is not always appreciated children who prefer spontaneity and child-centered activities.

Even family togetherness (seen by the ACoA as a marked improvement over the isolation of the alcoholic family) can be perceived as smothering by their children. The outcome may be occasional laughter and good times, but with an absence of real joy and pleasure in one another's company. The lack of choice and the climate of rigidity may lead children to believe that they need to act "as if this is fun" because Mom or Dad need me to enjoy it.

The inability to ask for help in an ACoA also impacts the way they parent their children and the environment created in the home. It must be remembered that they have a huge emotional investment in "making it different" from their alcoholic family of origin. They must be sure that the family they create in no way resembles the one they came from. The little self-esteem they have depends upon their ability to "pull it off".

As problems occur in normal family life, the ACoA has an exaggerated reaction, no matter how minor the problem and she will either fix and control the situation, or deny that the problem exists. Talking it over, depending upon others outside of the family, seeking help from friends or professionals represents a public admission of failure. Children of the ACoA are discouraged from pointing out or causing such problems but more importantly they must protect the family image. This need to preserve an image is much more than a superficial desire to look good to the community. The self-esteem of the ACoA parent depends upon keeping the secret that "we too have difficulties".

Family Secrets

One of the best kept family secrets with ACoA parents is their own family history. Rarely do the grandchildren of alcoholics know that there is alcoholism in the family. Situations and occurrences, which in another family would seem like meaningless events with no emotional charge attached, are to ACoAs shameful and embarrassing. For instance, temporary financial setbacks, health problems, divorce or remarriage may be kept secret for generations in an alcoholic family.

Ironically, in the chemically dependent or co-dependent family system there is less shame attached to being dysfunctional than there is in asking for help. Many recovering alcoholics who are grandchildren of alcoholics never tell their ACoA parent about their recovery. There are several reasons for this fear of disclosure, but among them is the shame of having a problem which they could not control themselves without help.

The tendency to think in extremes, One and Ten, Black and White, Right and Wrong, leads the ACoA parent who wants everything to be okay, to go underground with most conflicts. Needing instant approval or forgiveness, they prefer the easier but less complete solutions to problems.

After a serious argument when harsh words were exchanged, the whole family might be treated to a trip to the park or a pizza party. The incident would not be discussed by anyone and the feelings associated would be repressed. When arguments do occur, it is clear that there is a winner and a loser, someone is right (usually the most dominant or abusive) and someone is wrong. It may appear vital to an ACoA parent to prove his/her point and he may persist until the other party gives in, admitting fault.

The issue of blame is one that is a theme in a chemically dependent family. It also reflects the extreme thinking and low self-worth of the family system. ACoAs continue to seek a scapegoat to explain their own discomfort. Frequently, as in life with active addiction, the family appears to take sides, the same sides, on every issue. There are bad guys and good guys, and everyone knows who they are. Once labeled, it may be very difficult to break out of an expected behavior pattern.

SUMMARY

The damage to children raised in alcoholic homes has become much more widely realized in the field of chemical dependency, and is gaining attention in the general public through the media. However, our own denial has led to the belief that the negative effects are primarily a result of being around drinking behavior. ACoAs who do not become alcoholic themselves are demonstrating that the patterns of behavior and emotional unmanageability continue.

In their sincere efforts to create a family unlike the one they were raised in, Adult Children of Alcoholics eliminate the obvious negative behaviors and create the appearance of health. The absence of unconditional love, open expression of feelings and other necessary ingredients leave their children, the Grandchildren of Alcoholics, without adequate preparation for life, thus repeating the same negative patterns in their adult lives. The characteristics of Adult Children listed above become obstacles to good parenting and contribute to the growth of another generation of co-dependents, the Grandchildren of Alcoholics.

_____Chapter 2_____

Who Are
The Grandchildren
Of Alcoholics?

My personal interviews with Grandchildren of Alcoholics gave me an opportunity to hear the stories of six
individuals who had never before been able to explain
the dynamics of their family of origin without feeling as
though they were exaggerating or "making it up". A
common thread seems to be the need to protect the
image of the okay family while feeling internally that
something was drastically wrong.

The hours spent sharing how it was to be raised by
untreated Adult Children of Alcoholics were a healing
time for myself and those interviewed. The validation
that something really was wrong and that their personal
struggles today are related to those of their ACoA
parents was comforting and affirming. Almost every
Grandchild I asked to complete a questionnaire (to be

summarized in Chapter 3) agreed to be interviewed for my research. This response in itself told me that they want to talk and want others to know about the stories of Grandchildren. Those I was able to interview, eagerly gave their permission for this information to be included in a book reaching other GCoAs.

Joanne

Joanne is a 28-year-old woman who through her involvement in the 12-step program of Overeaters Anonymous became aware of treatment for Adult Children of Alcoholics. During her treatment she reported identifying with other Adult Children who talked openly at OA meetings about the "laundry list" of characteristics (described in Janet Woititz *Adult Children of Alcoholics)* and believed that since her parents were compulsive overeaters, the impact on her life must be similar. Friends recommended ACoA treatment and Joanne, who is committed to her own growth, followed their advice. Until she entered inpatient ACoA treatment, Joanne was unaware of the direct impact of alcoholism on her family and her own life.

In addition to her problems with compulsive overeating from which she was recovering, Joanne also reported difficulties in her relationships plus struggles with depression and anxiety. She described herself as having very low self-worth and an inability to feel. Her relationships with her family of origin were improving as a result of her involvement in Overeaters Anonymous, but were still painful and strained.

Joanne, not presently in an intimate relationship, had had a two-year live-in relationship in the past and several short-term "very painful" relationships since. She was feeling some internal pressure to start a family, although she was not feeling ready or able to do that. Joanne was comfortable with herself in her chosen career but feelings of inadequacy continued. Joanne was the third child, oldest girl, of nine children. She had three brothers and five sisters, and describes herself as a "lost child". Her mother was an Adult Child with an alcoholic father. The family never talked about it as alcoholism, just that "It was always joked about. They used to carry him (her grandfather) out of a bar . . . He always put on lots of parties." Joanne strongly suspects that her father's father was also alcoholic, but as is common in the alcoholic family, it was never directly stated. Her father's dysfunctional behavior strongly resembled that of an ACoA.

She described him as someone who was extremely rigid, always knowing the "right answers". "We were supposed to think and feel like him. I remember one time I expressed an opinion about something and he slapped me in the face and said, 'I want you to stop having these crazy thoughts and crazy ideas.' " Her father was dominant and in control "with his silence, withdrawal, depression, outbursts, poor health and whining." He did not drink or use drugs, but used food and work to medicate feelings which were rarely expressed.

Joanne's mother was described as passive and unavailable.

"She went to the hospital a lot for different things, operations and babies. She was away when I started my period. I felt ashamed and didn't want anyone to know, and also I really felt abandoned by my mother and wanted her to be there for me. I felt really scared because there was so much I didn't know about it. They never told me."

Joanne's mother was focused on her husband's moodiness, keeping the peace, feeding, clothing and disciplining the children, trying to keep everyone "good and quiet". The anger she could not safely vent with her husband would come out on the children in the form of slapping. Another playful side was occasionally visible but quickly suppressed in favor of seriousness. Joanne's family looked normal or even better than average to the outside world. There was never any active addiction in the home. According to Joanne, they were "a good Catholic family, happy, well-fed and well-dressed who stuck together through thick and thin."

On weekends her family spent a lot of time in the outdoors together, taking walks, going on hikes, skating in the winter, taking long rides in the summer. Joanne suspected that her father, who initiated these family activities, was doing it because he thought he was supposed to, rather than for the fun of it. All activities were centered around what he wanted to do. At times he appeared "almost abusive" to the children, for instance, when taking all-day rides on weekends which were long and exhausting. Everyone was forced to go to church on Sundays with no discussion of why they were doing it.

In contrast to the "happy family" image projected externally, Joanne felt isolated and unhappy.

"I believe that I really got the sense that it was not okay to be sad or to cry because I always did it alone, and there was never any support or comfort."

Despite having a large family, Joanne and her brothers and sisters never cried or expressed feelings in front of each other. After one of her father's angry outbursts, hitting and screaming, he would then be sweet and gentle and expect everyone to forget the whole thing. Joanne didn't forget, but she also did not talk about it in an effort to keep the peace. Her repressed anger grew into hatred for him, which she hid and felt guilty about.

Joanne rebelled by not cooperating with household responsibilities. Her father's reaction to any resistance was to hit with a belt "until it hurt". Her fear of his physical abuse drove Joanne further into her lost child role. Anger was replaced with silence whenever uncomfortable feelings were experienced.

Although there was no real sharing, affection or intimacy between family members, there was laughter and the appearance of having a good time. Joanne always sensed the distance despite the appearance of togetherness. She observed distance between her parents and swore it would never happen in her relationships, but she states today, "It always seemed so strange to me and I said that it would never happen to me but it has, and it (the isolation) always has been there."

Although Joanne's family did normal things together, laughed and played, they were unable to really connect with each other or anyone else. The marriage that served as a model for Joanne's future relationships was one of dependence, yet isolation and distance. She did not witness any sharing, affection or even problem-solving and thus found herself repeating these dysfunctional patterns in her adolescent and adult life.

Our interview was conducted after she had completed her five-and-one-half day ACoA treatment and at that time Joanne was much relieved to find out that she was not unique and that her family had been affected by alcoholism for several generations.

"I feel a lot of relief knowing what it (co-dependency) is, knowing that there's help, that it can get better, that I don't have to be unhappy all my life, that there are so many wonderful people out there sharing the same problem and that we are all going to do it together."

Prior to entering ACoA treatment, Joanne feared not fitting in because she did not have an alcoholic parent. "I was real scared coming here . . .that I wouldn't be accepted and I didn't really plan on talking about my parents. I just didn't think people would understand . . . I've received a lot more understanding than I thought I would."

Joanne is committed to recovery and aware that although it is a long term process, she *can* be the person she wants to be.

Melissa

Melissa is a 24-year-old recovering alcoholic with three years sobriety in Alcoholics Anonymous. Although her parents were not chemically dependent, she was raised in a home with an alcoholic grandmother, her father's mother. Melissa sought treatment in the Adult Children of Alcoholics program because she identified with other ACoAs and believed her difficulties were related to the alcoholism in her family.

Melissa is single but has been in a serious relationship with a man for the past few months. She reports having three very dysfunctional relationships prior to this. At 16 she was involved with a man 10 years older who was verbally and physically abusive, breaking her nose twice. She remained in this relationship for over three years. Both were active alcoholics at the time.

Within weeks Melissa had moved in with another man, who she described as "nice but boring". He was the child of an alcoholic, having been abused himself. She left him after seven months, and at that point began her recovery in AA.

Her relationships resulted in three abortions and uncontrollable anxiety attacks. Her hypochondria finally brought her to the point of seeking help. She suffers from chronic depression, which she describes as a "general feeling of unhappiness", regardless of the good things in her life.

Melissa is the eldest of two children. Her brother (one year younger), also a recovering alcoholic, stopped drinking one year earlier than Melissa. They were raised in the home of their paternal Grandmother who lived with them, despite her active alcoholism and abusive behavior.

Melissa's mother was a teacher, while her father was described as unable to work. He did not have any physical disability but had difficulty getting along with his employers. When asked at school in front of classmates what her father did, Melissa told them he was a writer. She was very embarrassed by his unemployment and began to cover up for her family. She describes her father as totally dysfunctional emotionally and her mother as helpless and passive. "Nobody ever told us anything. Nobody ever said do your homework, go to bed on time, eat a good breakfast, finish your dinner. Nothing, never any direction."

The environment Melissa lived in was chaotic and abusive. There was no discipline, no affection, no parenting.

Melissa's father was raised in an alcoholic home. His parents were divorced when he was five years old. His mother was a functional alcoholic, working very hard to support the family, but drinking daily and "getting smashed every night".

During his childhood and adult life his mother had many relationships with men, all of them dysfunctional. His father was also alcoholic and co-dependent, frequently a victim of his mother's abuse. Being an only child, Melissa's father felt obligated to maintain his connection with his mother, despite the damaging effects on his life and his family. He became a compulsive gambler, chronically depressed and was dysfunctional as a parent and husband.

Melissa has very little information about her mother, except that she was raised to be a strict Catholic, became pregnant and got married even though she didn't want to. Melissa's mother told her that she would have had an abortion if she could. This pregnancy resulted in Melissa's being born, unwanted and later abused. She does not remember ever being touched by her mother.

Although her parent's were aware and acknowledged her grandmother's excessive drinking, they never confronted it but instead would argue with each other. The option of moving into a home of their own was not considered. Her grandmother's drinking directly impacted Melissa as well, in the form of verbal and physical abuse.

Eventually, Melissa and her brother became abusive to their grandmother, calling her names and once even throwing eggs at her.

Her mother wanted to leave when Melissa and her brother were very young but always found reasons to postpone the decision. The children begged her to leave and talked openly about their contempt for their father. They resorted to calling him names and making fun of him. The fighting and contempt continued until Melissa was eight years old. She recalls an incident which changed everything for her.

"All of a sudden he was a time bomb, he exploded at me. We were watching TV, having a good time when I said he had dandruff. He threw me up against a chair, beat the shit out of me, called me horrible names and said he wanted to kill me. Mom had to pull him off me, and after that he wouldn't talk to me for five months."

From that point on, Melissa lived in fear. Where no limits had been set for her or her brother until this incident, violence became the threat to keep her in line. She never again felt safe to express her feelings or opinions. Feeling powerless to change anything, she resorted to extreme acting out and using chemicals and sex to escape.

During the period that Melissa's addiction was progressing, her parents tried to alleviate the situation by telling her they cared for her and that she could come to them with any problems. She did not believe them and responded by becoming more rebellious. Their solution was to put her in a psychiatric hospital off and on during her adolescence.

With Melissa's involvement in AA, their relationship is improving, but it remains very superficial. Ironically, her parents who never took care of themselves are now addicted to sports: tennis, exercise, etc. They did not speak to her brother for two years until recently on their

25th anniversary where the whole family went to dinner to "celebrate".

Melissa and her brother are close today, but she does not feel she really knows him.

Without any sense of what "normal" is, Melissa is hopeful that with professional help and AA, she will continue to grow and eventually have a healthy life. She is now entering a human service position and would like to reach out to other co-dependents when she is ready to give it away.

Harriet

Harriet, age 53, is a recovering alcoholic who recently discovered that her paternal grandfather was also alcoholic. Until this discovery, Harriet believed that although alcoholism was a disease for "other"people, she personally had brought it on herself out of her own weakness. Since she knew of no other alcoholics in her family and unlike many of her friends in AA, she could not call herself an ACoA, Harriet felt totally responsible for her alcoholism.

A great deal of healing has taken place in Harriet's life as a result of examining her family history. She now has six years sobriety which began after the death of her parents.

Harriet is a single woman, a retired elementary school teacher who has never been married or in a serious intimate relationship. She states that she has always lived at home and continues to do so today. She was the eldest of two children, having a brother seven years younger. Harriet describes her father, the ACoA, as kind, loving and supportive, while her mother was angry, aloof and cold. She readily admits that she has difficulty seeing her father as in any way responsible for her painful childhood since her perception of him was always as the "good guy" in the family.

Externally, her family was highly respected in the community, due to her father's position as high school administrator. Both parents were active socially, playing bridge, belonging to community organizations and church. They regularly took family vacations to the ocean, camping and fishing. Harriet reported that her mother's two unmarried sisters generally went along on any family excursions. Much like Joanne, Harriet's father initiated many rides in the car on Sundays, and her comment was similarly, that she felt he did this because he was supposed to, rather than because anyone enjoyed it.

In sharp contrast, Harriet painfully described the emotional void in which she grew up. Although her physical needs were more than adequately met, Harriet remembers an awareness at the age of four or five that her mother did not love her. Her father began to compensate for the lack of nurturing by becoming extremely attentive and assumed the role of caretaker for she and her brother.

Harriet began to act out the repressed emotion in the family through rebellion and extreme jealousy of her brother. She recalls with guilt that her angry behavior towards him included physical abuse.

Feelings were never shared although a great deal of discussion took place. Harriet never cried in front of her parents or brother, and never saw anyone else cry. There was no touching or affection expressed. Secrets were felt but rarely discussed. Harriet recalled that her father had an affair when she was a teenager. He was not overly discreet about it, and would see the other woman occasionally when her mother was around. She remembers that her mother didn't like the woman but there was never an argument or discussion between her parents. Despite her discomfort with the situation, Harriet never asked her father about it.

Harriet vividly remembers the coldness and distance of her mother. She has no knowledge of addiction in this family but commented frequently that her mother's siblings were called "crazy". They were enmeshed in the sense that they spent an unusual amount of time together, and as a rule, women in that family did not marry or have intimate relationships outside of the family.

Her mother's two sisters lived nearby and were a part of Harriet's family until they died in 1965 and 1966. Harriet then became closer to her mother until her death just before Harriet began her sobriety.

As a child she reports wanting desperately to please her mother. "I can remember as a child, saying to her 'Why don't you say something to me?' Begging to know why she was angry with me." Her mother's response was to withdraw further. After being hit once by her mother, Harriet recalls that her father became furious at her mother, telling her never to hit Harriet again, which she did not.

Although her relationship with her father was significantly better, Harriet did not experience closeness with him either. She remembers many times in her childhood when her father intervened on her behalf but there were more occasions when she needed him emotionally, and he was not able to respond.

One incident reflecting his good intentions, but inability to connect, occurred when Harriet was in college. In a letter following Harriet's sharing with him her homesickness on being away at college for the first time, he advised her that he did not want to interfere in her life in any way and that if she had any problems, she should pray to God. The letter and advice in themselves demonstrated to Harriet that he cared, but once again he was unable to offer himself for her support.

Today Harriet feels a sense of loss when she reflects on the years of loneliness and isolation. She finds herself unable to form intimate relationships, and even within AA she is known to be secretive. Having recently received treatment for addiction and co-dependency, she is hopeful that she can begin to change this lifetime pattern.

Steve

At the age of 46, Steve has had two years of recovery in AA. He has been separated from his wife for the past six years, feeling torn about the possibility of divorce. He has three children in their 20s, and was a successful businessman even in his addiction to cocaine and alcohol. Today in his recovery, he is considering a career change, working as a counselor with other addicts.

Although Steve exhibits the serenity of new sobriety, he is fearful of digging into a painful past which he has avoided until now.

Steve's father was an Adult Child with an alcoholic father. His father immigrated here from Italy when he was in his 30s and Steve never met his grandfather. It was common knowledge in his family that this grandfather died of alcoholism. His mother's father was also known to "drink a lot" but Steve is not sure it was alcoholism. The results this may have had on his parents or the next generation were never discussed.

Steve was the fourth child of five, the youngest for eleven years until his sister was born. He was treated as very special, a family mascot, and to a great extent was parented by his older brothers and sisters in his father's absence. He feels they spoiled him a lot by giving him gifts, keeping him with them all the time. Steve believes they were trying to make it different for him than it had been for them growing up. All but one of his siblings today either lives with alcoholism, is alcoholic or has addicted children.

In describing his family of origin, Steve presents two very contrasting pictures. When he remembers his mother, he recalls a loving family where feelings were expressed, laughter shared and a great deal of togetherness enjoyed.

He states, "My mother is probably the most selfless, caring person you'd ever meet. We always knew that she was totally dedicated to her family . . . and demanded nothing for herself. She's a fine lady."

When he speaks of his father, he recalls abuse, criticism, angry control. "He resented having family obligations. He would let us know it . . . all the self-sacrifice that he had to do to provide for us and (he said) we weren't worth it. My reaction was just to avoid him, he didn't exist for me." His father would not permit playing and fun, and for a while would not even allow the family to celebrate Christmas, calling it "nonsense". The children were protected by their mother, whom Steve describes as a martyr, and they managed to have pleasant moments as a family when his father was not around.

When he reflects on the past, Steve states, "It's a shame. I feel a sense of loss with my brothers and sisters and myself, knowing how things could have been. I believe we have a lot of talent as a family. We have a good-looking family."

As other ACoAs also describe their family of origin, Steve's family presented a positive image to the outside world. "We were a very popular family. All of us had many friends and our cousins were kind of drawn to our family. We were the most popular family. We just kept quiet about what was really going on."

At the age of 10 Steve discovered a family secret which intensified his negative feelings about his father. He overheard a conversation where his mother was telling someone about his father's other wives.

Steve shared, "I was the first in my family to find out. I found out I had brothers and sisters in a foreign country, and there was another family in California. There were two children there. He never even bothered getting divorces."

Steve has kept the secret to this day, never talking about it, or telling his brothers or sisters, never questioning his father or mother. He is concerned and frightened about what effect this may have had on him as an adult. Steve was determined, as many ACoAs are, that he would never be like his father, but in his own role as husband and father, he found himself repeating the same patterns of behavior which he despised.

Steve married a woman he describes as "just like my mother . . . She came from a very loving, very normal functioning family . . . Why she felt bad about herself, I don't know, she had the perfect childhood, perfect parents." Steve's wife never confronted his addiction, even though she believed it was wrong. She was willing to sacrifice her life if necessary for the marriage. Steve, following the modeling of his father, became dominating, angry and abusive. He was unable to share any feeling openly, with the exception of anger.

His relationships with his children were authoritarian and controlling, rather than supportive and loving. He was frequently compared to his father, which hurt badly. Steve believes he may have been too strict with his children, but that despite his father's poor example, Steve did a better job at parenting than his father. Eventually Steve began to have affairs, as his father had done, and coupled with his addiction to cocaine, his family deteriorated.

Steve's recovery from addiction during the last two years has not been easy. He utilizes Alcoholics Anonymous, and with the 12 steps has been able to make strides in his relationships with his children and his own self-esteem. He remains uncertain about his marriage and is fearful of the feelings which may arise if he begins to look at his painful childhood.

Roy

At 29 Roy describes himself as having "jobaphobia", a very poor work history, frequent depression and anxiety, a spending addiction and chemical dependency. He is beginning his recovery in most of these areas but recognizes the difficulties ahead. Roy is the grandchild of an alcoholic.

His mother was raised in a very abusive alcoholic home. He only discovered this information when she died 18 months ago. Roy's maternal grandmother was responsible for him and his sister and brothers until she died when he was six years old. He describes her as a very angry woman who "ruled with an angry fist". His father, a workaholic, was raised in a dysfunctional home. This may have been related to the workaholism in running a family business for many generations.

Roy's parents owned a catering business in a small community. As the only business of its kind in that area, it was well known and respected. His mother and father were of the belief that a good family works hard, takes care of their children and does not do frivolous things like play.

Roy recalls his mother complaining to his father about the constant hard work and lack of joy in their lives. She was forced to work in the business after she married his father and strongly objected. Despite her anger, they continued to center their lives around work, having a housekeeper and other relatives taking care of the children while they maintained the business. There were rare moments when they were together as a family.

Roy describes his father as a "cynical, quiet, sarcastic" person with a "silent abusiveness". He had very high expectations of his children, particularly his sons, and was extremely critical when they were not met.

Roy was the youngest of four children and fits the pattern of a family mascot detailed by Sharon Weg-scheider-Cruse in *Another Chance*. As the last born after a seven-year gap, Roy was encouraged to be cute and precocious. He was exceptionally intelligent, a quality that was found entertaining to his parents and siblings, and was asked to perform for them frequently.

He explained, "I was like a show. I was a circus. Roy was the circus, who was put on a little stage to multiply. I remember being given pads of paper and doing arithmetic for people at three years old. I could do no wrong and got what I wanted by screaming and yelling."

As a mascot, Roy was rarely disciplined and to a large extent grew up with no limits. In reaction to this, he became hyperactive and a problem child in school, unable to remain seated or attentive, extremely disorganized and sloppy, and a distraction to other students.

Coming from dysfunctional backgrounds, his parents had no tools with which to create the healthy family they sought. Roy recalls his father saying (referring to the Andy Griffith show on television), "If you could be like Opie, that would be very good. Why can't you be like Opie?"

His brother and sister, who were twins, brought self-esteem to the family through success and popularity in school. Roy, who was unable to do this, began to act out. At one point he knew he was out of control and asked for help, but his family refused to seek counseling for him.

Little or no affection was ever shown in Roy's family, instead love was shown through material things. Every summer the children were sent to camp until school resumed. Roy had difficulty surviving the structured activities of camp and begged his parents to let him stay home but they believed they were giving him the best care they could due to their absences from work demands. When Roy was young they attempted to control him with money, giving him things to get him to behave appropriately. When his parents cut him off financially in later years, Roy resorted to stealing from them.

When Roy was in high school, things began to deteriorate at home. His mother who had frequently been angry in the past, became very depressed and abusive. She started to use medication, sleeping pills and tranquilizers to cope.

Roy recalls, "She would stay in bed a lot, watching television. It was either that or complete hysteria, screaming and yelling 'What are you doing to my young life? Sending me to an early grave? I can't stand this anymore, what do you want from me?' It was always her, it was always about her and what you were doing to her. There was never any recognition that maybe you had a problem." Until Roy was 16, his mother was physically abusive to him. At that point he threatened to hit her back and she stopped.

Roy's father continued to work compulsively, ignoring any problems at home. When describing his relationship with his father, Roy states, "I hated him. We hated each other. The older I got, the more of a failure I was to him. The more I didn't become what he wanted, the more my older brother became the Hero. When he (father) died, I was happy that I finally felt some freedom from this horrible oppressor who had dragged me down and made me feel like an invalid human."

Prior to adult children of alcoholics treatment, Roy described himself as "feeling completely non-functional". He is beginning to understand that he is only one of the victims in generations of co-dependency and chemical dependency within his family. In addition to his obvious co-dependency, Roy must now face his addiction to drugs and alcohol and a spending addiction. Unfortunately, Roy has a great deal to learn about living as a responsible adult, but with appropriate professional help and a healthy support system, he is hopeful for his recovery.

David

David is a psychotherapist in private practice. At 49 he is in his third marriage and has one daughter from his first marriage. His mother, now deceased, was the child of an alcoholic father. His father was not from an alcoholic family but exhibited the signs of having been from a dysfunctional system.

The fact that his mother was an Adult Child was not openly discussed in the family, but David's grandfather was described as one who enjoyed "bending the elbow". His mother was extremely close to her father. Prior to her marriage to David's father, she was a successful nursing supervisor.

Although his father was not from an alcoholic family, David's uncle and several other family members became or married alcoholics. There have been comments by other family members that David's grandfather had a spending compulsion and used money recklessly.

David's parents did not drink excessively when he was a young child, but began to use alcohol and other drugs when he was about 10 years old. David was an only child, and describes a very painful and isolated childhood, even before the drinking began. Until very recently David was unaware that alcoholism had anything to do with the problems in his family. His professional training did not include alcoholism until the past year, and his personal insight is very new despite years of intensive therapy.

David's father was a physician who was a workaholic. His mother, having been a nurse, centered her life around her husband and his practice, which was in their home. According to David, his parents portrayed themselves as "exceptional, wonderful people . . . better than the best. They had the best marriage and they worked very hard." They were highly respected as a family in the community, but David was very aware of the deficiences in their family life.

His parents, particularly his mother, were extremely dependent on each other, to the exclusion of their child. Part of their byword was, "We stick together through thick and thin, your father never does anything without me, I never do anything without him. We are like this, we will always be like this and nothing can ever come between us." They were a very proper, moral family, centered on medicine, patients and intellectual discussions.

David feels he was treated much like another one of their "cases", rather than as a wanted child. "My mother didn't hold me, she prided herself that I was only on a bottle for three days and that she got me on a cup. She had me potty trained when I was something like six months old."

David's mother was probably sexually addicted and he painfully describes her obsession with her own and his sexuality. As many victims of incest are inclined to do, David minimizes the impact of her sexual abuse.

David's father was away for five years during the war. His mother turned her dependence toward David, even though she continued to write letters to her husband several times a day. He recalls his mother's behavior, "I don't think I was ever physically abused, I think I was emotionally neglected. My mother was very, very seductive. She would come in the bathroom, while I was there, and wanted to wash my body particularly my genitals, and comment about them. She also talked a great deal about her own body, showing me her genitals, explaining where everything was . . ."

Her practice of tucking him in at night, crying and telling him how much she loved him continued into David's adult life.

David describes his father as a very unemotional, overly critical, angry man. "My father was a cold and distant man, but was known as a kind, gentle, loving doctor, which he sure wasn't at home. His response when my mother complained about his being unemotional was 'I'm a physician, I can't afford to feel, if I feel, I'll go to pieces. I will not be vulnerable, no one will make me feel, I am a scientist.' "

Although he was extremely conscientious and well liked in his medical practice, he could be cruel in his treatment of his own son. On several occasions when David had injured himself, his father treated and stitched very painful wounds without anesthesia, having him bite on a tongue depressor instead. He would not have done this to any other patient. David grew to fear his father, yet continued to seek his approval.

In order to focus more totally on their work, David's parents put him in the care of a 12-year-old girl who came to live with them when he was a baby. She and an older housekeeper who was mentally retarded were the primary caregivers in the home.

Food became extremely important as a substitute for love and nurturing. "We had a minimum of two gigantic freezers, sometimes three. The pantry was the size of a large room and was stocked like a restaurant. The reward was always food."

As David grew up he became more unacceptable to his parents. Although his father wanted him to become a doctor, David chose to become a minister, a profession his father considered useless.

He married a woman who was in need of rescuing from her own painful family. He gradually became abusive to her over their eight year relationship. He divorced her after having an affair and quickly married again. Despite years of therapy, during the first and second marriage, David could not sustain any degree of self-esteem nor manage to relate in a healthy way with those he cared about. His new wife began and continued an affair with a close friend of David's for seven years. David was aware of the affair and did little to stop it or take care of himself.

Although they appeared functional professionally, David and his wife were living in "insanity". He too began to have affairs while seeking the help of therapists to straighten out the mess. In defeat David eventually left his wife and lived alone for four years.

As an extremely intelligent and analytical person, much like his parents, David has mananged to figure out "why" he has done everything, but has yet to come to terms with the emotional impact of his painful childhood and adult life.

Six years ago, he married for the third time, again taking a caretaker role for a troubled woman. This relationship, however, led both to reach out for appropriate help to seek personal growth and real change. They too have had major struggles, coping with both of their painful histories, the difficulties of blended families, step-children, etc.

David comments about his present and future, "My feeling about me is that I survived and I'm proud of me for doing that. I'm still not where I want to be and I've still got a lot of unsettled business in this belly of mine, but I've managed to take care of myself and to be helpful to lots of people and that to me feels like it ought to be."

SUMMARY

Prior to my interviews, I had not anticipated the severe abuse reported by these Grandchildren. I was struck by the inability of ACoA and other dysfunctional parents to respond to the needs of their children. It is clear that despite the development of chemical dependence in some of their parents in later years, all six were born into a co-dependent family system. Each had parents with good intentions and strong motivations to make their family different from those they were raised in. Each parent tried to change the external signs to convince themselves and the world that they were okay while their internal suffering continued.

_____CHAPTER 3_____

Characteristics Common to Grandchildren of Alcoholics and Their Families

To discover the characteristics common to Grand-children of Alcoholics (GCoAs), I surveyed 100 Grand-children of Alcoholics over the age of 18, who did not have an alcoholic parent when they were growing up. I found them in professional workshops, conferences and in treatment for co-dependency due to a present relationship or recovery from their own addiction. Grandchildren of Alcoholics as a group do not readily identify themselves as such, most never having examined the issue prior to their treatment and/or training.

As I present this information at workshops and conferences in my role as a trainer/educator in the co-dependency field, I am struck by the overwhelming response of the Grandchildren at finally being identified. They are grateful for the validation of someone saying something was wrong, you did not imagine it, you are entitled to help.

Summary of Survey

Family Description

Several patterns appeared as Grandchildren responded to questions about themselves and their families. Although every home was unique, some extremely abusive, others appearing to be the "ideal" family, underneath it all the Grandchildren experienced very similar thoughts and feelings. The things these families had in common follow:

75% Never Told About Grandparent's Alcoholism

Most Grandchildren had parents who drew a curtain on the past and did not ever talk about their family history in negative terms. Those who were told reported that it was too obvious to deny. When talking with GCoAs, it is amazing how little they know about the family they came from. Many are aware of alcoholic aunts and uncles and may have accidentally uncovered a grandparent's addiction through a more distant relative. Some reported overhearing conversations or just putting pieces of the puzzle together over a period of years.

They made their discoveries as adults, most very recently, and remain fearful of bringing it up around their parents. When they begin a search for family history, they meet with resistance and fear in other family members and often discover that no one in the family has the whole picture. It is interesting to note that until they are questioned specifically about their families, most Grandchildren do not realize that they don't know much. They have not even noticed that there is an absence of detailed information. They have never questioned why that is the case.

95% of ACoA Parents Did Not Acknowledge Being Affected by their Parents' Alcoholism

Almost all of the parents of the GCoAs believed they could erase the past and be undamaged by childhood pain and abuses. They were especially insistent that the past would in no way affect the way they parent their children. They (the ACoA parent) felt that since the drinking person was no longer present in their home today, the problem no longer existed.

Many ACoAs never acknowledge, even in their own minds, that a parent was alcoholic, and so are unable to have insight about its negative effects on their childhood or adult life. They did not consciously deny problems. They, like the alcoholic, were "sincerely deluded", believing that "It will never happen to me."

The desire to maintain control at all times is a powerful force for the ACoA parent. They believe intellectually that they can think this through, learn from their parents' mistakes and do it differently with sheer will power. They see healthy family life as something they can decide to do, and "pull off", without any modeling, tools or training.

90% Report the Presence of Some Addiction Other than Chemicals in the Family

Although chemical dependency may not be present in the families of GCoAs, repressed feelings are acted out through "other" addictions and/or compulsions. The ACoA parent, who was raised with the model of compulsive behavior in both the addicted and the non-addicted parent, knows no other way to deal with the pain they were not able to express. They continue these patterns and bring them into their new family system as adults.

64% reported workaholism as the most common compulsion in one or both parents.

28% reported parents or siblings being addicted to food (many had both food and work).

Others identified cleaning (10%), spending (9%), perfectionism (9%), gambling (5%) and caretaking (4%).

Workaholism is considered a "positive addiction" in today's society and fathers who are ACoAs view it as "taking care of the family". The GCoAs sees only the fact that a parent was absent and assumes that work is more important than children. The ACoA parents are concerned with doing the right thing, looking good to the world and doing a better job than their parents did.

Food may be seen as a means of soothing hurt feelings, and rewarding and celebrating good things. Often in dysfunctional families it becomes a means of nurturing oneself or others in the absense of the real thing. Many GCoAs talk about food being the center of their lives and family activities. Food was used to say "I love you", "I'm sorry," "You did a good job".

In time use of food as a sedative or mood elevator becomes progressively more compulsive. Family members may binge uncontrollably and struggle with compulsive overeating and obesity. Grandchildren may also use refusal to eat as a means of expressing repressed anger.

80% of GCoAs Were Told Repeatedly that They Had a "Good Family"

GCoAs were often told verbally and directly that their family was special. Several were told they were better than other families, e.g., more fortunate, had better parents, a happier home, better education, etc. They were told how lucky they were that they had everything they needed. They were reminded that "We don't fight", "We don't drink" like those other people. Most Grandchildren reported an "over-kill" of family praise to the point where it was no longer believable. Image and outward appearance were vitally important and protected.

Pride, loyalty and family unity were well taught. Many described the mandatory family gatherings, vacations, outings, etc., with no regard for personal choice. Family mottos were shared, for example, "We can beat anything together", "If we can't help each other, no one else will", "It's us against the world".

Many GCoAs sensed the contradiction between what they were told, and what they saw and experienced but were not able to express this.

20% of GCoAs Felt Loved, Despite the Fact that 80% Were Told They Were Loved, and 54% Had "Loving Things" Done in their Families

Words of love were spoken in most of the GCoA families and yet very few felt or believed this love. The ACoA parents made sincere efforts to act loving and to say the right things, but were incapable through expression of their own vulnerability to be intimate with their children. Their loving acts were usually in the form of material things, vacations, over-attentiveness or over-protecting which they viewed as overt expression of their affection for their children. These efforts were interpreted by the GCoA as an attempt to pacify or buy them off, rather than spending time actually getting to know them as unique persons. Parents were so busy "doing it right" that they neglected the emotional needs of their children. Although the GCoA in some cases knows intellectually that their parent loves them, they are unable to feel it internally, "in their gut". They are eager to give parents credit for their effort to do it, but have to admit that it often didn't "get in" for them.

The ACoA fear of abandonment prevents him or her from risking with their child by asking questions like "What do you need? How do you feel?" because they fear that they will not be able to handle the answer. If a child responds by saying "I need you to accept me for who I am", the parent has no idea how to do that, since they have never experienced such acceptance themselves.

More important than the praise for accomplishments and achievement is how the parent reacts to a child's failures or "down" times. These are the moments children remember when they question whether they were loved. Many GCoAs lived with perfectionistic, critical parents, who with the motive of love, tried to mold character and protect their children from future problems by constantly teaching and correcting. The result is that the child feels the effort of the parent and interprets this as "They would love me if only I were better. It must be my fault". The truth is that love will not be accepted or "absorbed" unless it is given unconditionally.

Characteristics Of The Adult Grandchild Of an Alcoholic

As a group Grandchildren strongly resemble Adult Children of Alcoholics. 97% identify with the standard lists of ACoA Characteristics. Prior to completing the questionnaire for my research, all had either read or heard a description of the Adult Child from an accepted authority in this field. Many were baffled by the fact that they so closely related to the ACoA "syndrome". The list of characteristics will probably be shared by some ACoAs, especially those raised in "looking good" families. However, they are more familiar to

Grandchildren and are designed to give them something to identify with so that they may begin to connect their present with their past.

1. Distorted Family Image

GCoAs have distorted images of their own families, unable to see anything wrong, despite evidence to the contrary. Grandchildren often rave about how good their childhood was, while they themselves are dysfunctional as adults. Those who make it to AA or Al-Anon through their own or a loved one's addiction, find they do not identify with others from troubled homes, and frequently talk about how good they had it as children. They are not able to attribute any of their present difficulties to their family background.

They become positively deluded with "rose-colored glasses" and may develop a pattern, similar to the Adult Child who does not notice dysfunction or insanity around him. They are accustomed to living in two realities, and inside one and an outside one, and no longer trust their own instincts. They can smile and say things are great when they are really hurting inside.

Because of this learned ability to ignore pain, they may be surrounded with people in crises and believe they are unaffected by it. They do not seek help because they do not have a problem. In their intimate relationships Grandchildren may find themselves taking the role of the "all-together" one who others depend upon. They may also appear arrogant or superior and find themselves isolated because they look "too good". In their marriages, GCoAs may be overly defensive about their families, unwilling to admit to even slight human flaws. 76% identified with having a distorted family image.

2. Self-Blaming

When their lives become unmanageable, they blame themselves (66%). Without the connection to the past which many Adult Children have, the GCoA may attribute their problems, character defects and poor choices to their own inability to function as an adult. They look back and see a seemingly healthy family system, parents who did their best to prepare them for the world, and they conclude, "There must be something wrong with me." Some of the comments of GCoAs demonstrate this.

"I felt I was the only sick one in the family."

"I was crazy; they were normal."

"I was treated like an outcast by my family. Everyone looked okay but me. I believed it was my fault, and so did they."

"I believed if I could only be more like them, more together, more successful, I would be all right."

"I felt my family was loving and caring. It must be my fault if I felt different or acted out."

"I could never share my pain, ask for help or comfort because I was told I was to blame for my own problems, and I knew my mother would be so ashamed."

These Grandchildren know that the self-esteem of their families and their parents depends on how they perform and therefore feel a great deal of shame at not bringing pride to the family. Many were given the message as they were growing up that their parents could not, or would not, handle the guilt of having made any mistakes, so the GCoA assumed full responsibility for turning out less than perfect. In adult life when they find themselves married to a chemically dependent person, or having an addicted child, they blame themselves and are reluctant to even share these problems with their parents and siblings for fear of judgment or criticism.

3. Good At Forming Superficial Relationships

Eighty percent of GCoAs are very good at forming superficial relationships but struggle with anything resembling intimacy. Chemically dependent families, out of necessity, keep many secrets about family history, skeletons in the past and about who they really are as people. Children with critical parents learn at a very early age that it is not safe to be who you are, and will begin to figure out what is acceptable, silencing the "real person", as young as two or three years old. Coming from low self-esteem, they learn to present to the world what they think it wants to see. The result is that a pseudo-self is created to protect the fragile self-esteem and gain the approval necessary for survival.

Grandchildren have been skillfully trained in this deception and become capable of convincing others that they are seeing the real thing. In relationships they will give just enough information to others to keep them around, but no one ever gets the whole picture:

"I had many friends as a child, and even as an adult, but I don't believe anyone really knew me. I only presented them with the positive side of me and was there as a support to them. I could talk and talk socially, but never really said anything important about myself. I was in a crowd, but always alone."

"All my life I was surrounded by people from alcoholic families. All my friends were struggling with something. I believed I came from a happy home and I could help them. This was the pattern of all my relationships and still is. I am the okay one who doesn't need anything."

If the GCoA lived in a home where intimacy was replaced with sociability, caretaking and image-consciousness, it follows that they would become skilled in these areas. Unless intimacy is modeled and a part of a healthy family system, children will be unable to create genuine intimacy. They may, in an attempt to connect and fit in, create pseudo-intimacy, mimicking the behaviors of true emotional connection, but having none of the feelings nor the ability to take the risks necessary for healthy relating.

4. Difficulty Asking For Help

Grandchildren of Alcoholics have extreme difficulty asking for help (90%). To the GCoA the mere fact of needing help means that they have done something wrong and should be able to fix it themselves.

Growing up with ACoA parents, most Grandchildren sensed the difficulty their parents had with considering even the possibility that their family resembled the one they came from. The game became "Let's pretend we are all happy, healthy, honest, open."

When children care for their parents, they naturally want to please them. If Mommy appears overwhelmed with guilt or disappointment when I bring her a problem, I won't have very many problems or I will learn not to tell her about them.

Grandchildren of alcoholics have not been asked what they need and have not learned to express their needs to others. Needing is seen as dependency and weakness, something to be ashamed of and avoided. Asking for help suggests that there is something wrong with you or with the family.

Often a parent will react by trying to fix the problem, giving quick answers, rather than allowing the child to learn from his or her mistakes, feeling supported through this process. ACoA parents have difficulty letting their children think for themselves and may out of their own need to control and prevent pain, sabotage this necessary step in the developmental process. The result for the GCoA is an inability to include the input and help of others when addressing difficult problems.

5. Struggle With Compulsive Behaviors

Compulsion (defined here as repeated action without choice) is common in Grandchildren of Alcoholics. Of those surveyed 81% report struggling with compulsive behaviors, for example, food, sex, work, relationships, smoking, spending, chemicals. As with their parents, the most frequently mentioned are work and food.

In any family system where feelings are repressed, they must be acted out behaviorially. When addiction to chemicals skips a generation, it does not eliminate the environment which is fertile for addiction. The family system continues to maintain the characteristics of a chemically dependent family and will support any addiction. Even if the addictions in the home are seemingly positive ones, like workaholism, the ACoA parents have modeled compulsive behavior, which is then picked up by the GCoA.

Ironically, despite the determination of Adult Children of Alcoholics to prevent alcohol abuse and addiction in their children, often they will have several or all of their children become chemically dependent. They cannot overcome the hereditary nature of the disease and are inclined to over-react and blame themselves when the disease appears in their children.

It has frequently been said that what parents do not deal with from their past, their children will continue to play out in *their* lives. This is apparent in the numerous addictions of Grandchildren of Alcoholics, who may carry a heavy burden of guilt for becoming dysfunctional out of a seemingly healthy family.

6. Tend To Be Secretive

Without any conscious awareness, GCoAs tend to be very secretive (86%). One person reported, "I tend to keep secrets myself. I knew I'd be in a lot of trouble if I ever talked about any of this."

Another describes her family, "They had secrets about things that were totally unimportant, who they were going to vote for, religious beliefs, age, etc., and also things that were very painful, especially when someone died, sexual things and alcoholism in general. I never quite knew what they were protecting, but I knew I shouldn't talk about these things." When questioned about their family histories, many GCoAs are surprised to discover how little they have been told.

The need to be secretive arises when there is the threat of abandonment, violence or serious harm if painful things are discussed. This is ingrained and becomes automatic to the ACoA, who then parents his or her children with this behavior. The need to protect each other from the truth is no longer as powerful, but children can sense what is upsetting and therefore taboo to their parents and will not feel free to talk openly as a result. They learn to share only what they must and rarely share outside the home. No one in the family acknowledges that this exists and children assume it is the "right" way to be, and so it continues as a way of life for the GCoA.

As an adult the GCoA has learned to function without "telling it all" to anyone. Painful events may come and go without even being mentioned to loved ones. It becomes easier to talk about neighbors, weather, news and other people's problems than about how one feels. The "trick" to this way of living is to stay very active and "busy" to avoid intimate moments with family or friends. While avoiding the pain and discomfort, however, the GCoA also misses out on the joy of being known and accepted by another human being.

7. Prone To Episodes Of Depression And Anxiety

Eighty percent of GCoAs report cyclical episodes of depression and/or anxiety. The unresolved pain and anger of the ACoA often shows itself in the form of unpredictable mood swings, much like that of the active alcoholic.

When listening to a description of the family of a Grandchild where no drinking was present, it is often difficult to detect any difference between the co-dependent family and the chemically dependent family. Many GCoAs live in fear of the emotional outbursts, rage and irrational mood swings of their parents.

The depression described by Grandchildren of Alcoholics is generally not severe "clinical depression". It is also not "situational depression", a reaction to negative circumstances. It appears that with the emotional repression in the family of origin, GCoAs have little or no release from anger, grief, hurts, etc., and turn these feelings inward. Over a period of years this repression, particularly of anger, shows itself in cyclical "down" periods, perhaps not extreme downs but a general feeling of powerlessness, isolation and sadness. These episodes, lasting days, weeks or even months, may be precipitated by a simple mistake, a minor disappointment or nothing at all. They may disappear as inexplicably as they appear.

The negative judgment of themselves, believing "I shouldn't feel this way", only pushes the GCoA further into the pain. They believe that unless the circumstances of their lives are as bad as other people, they have no right to their feelings.

The way out is not only learning to express the anger and other feelings, but also to become more accepting of themselves when they are "down", rather than looking for a justifiable explanation. If there were such an explanation, it would not lift the depression any sooner. Another important learning for many GCoAs is that above all else, they need to start talking about their pain.

Similar to the depressive cycle, Grandchildren report waves of anxiety which may range from momentary fears to full-blown panic attacks with the accompanying physical responses.

One GCoA shared, "I grew up anxious. I remember from childhood the phrase most often used when coming home from school, especially if I was late, I would go and find my brother and ask 'Is Dad mad?' ".

Another shared, "The only person allowed to express anger in my home was Dad. He could go crazy and we would all try to keep him happy. If one of us kids got mad, Dad's feelings would be hurt and he wouldn't talk to us for weeks. We learned not to get angry."

Many alternately experience anxiety and depression. They begin to build their lives around their fears, fears which may have been present since childhood. Excessive worry about events to come can deprive them of the moment they are in. When good things come, they have been warned by their ACoA parents not to trust them and so they sabotage the good in their lives by expecting it to disappear.

All children have fears but the response of the ACoA parent to that fear can frequently determine how long and how intense the feeling will be. The over-protective parent, working hard to "do it right", actually creates worry and fear by modeling it and teaching a child to be too careful.

The chemically dependent family generally lives by the axiom "If it feels good, do it compulsively. If it is uncomfortable, run the other way!"

As adults GCoAs will carry the childhood fears but go underground out of shame, covering their pain, adjusting their lives to avoid what frightens them. The outcome is a general fear of losing control, of becoming powerless, which of course happens to most of us every day.

The anxiety may grow, turning itself into cyclical panic attacks, which prevent normal functioning, e.g., leaving the house, driving a car, etc. This pattern can be one of extreme dependency, thus engendering a false sense of power and control over loved ones, who must become caretakers and protectors.

8. Strong Family Loyalty

Family loyalty is a powerful force in any chemically dependent system. 73% of GCoAs fear being disloyal to parents and family by admitting that their home life was less than ideal. 78% discount how poorly they were handled as children and give parents credit for "trying" rather than for what they actually did. Maintaining the myth that "We are a good family" (meaning, we have no problems) becomes of prime importance to some Grandchildren. They find themselves frequently defending their parents and siblings to others, even in a therapy setting.

One GCoA remembers breaking the family rule of don't talk negatively about the family. "The one time as an adult I dared to express my opinions about my family, my sister became angry and said 'Your perceptions are not accurate'.

"This is the story of my life. I needed their approval more than I needed to be honest with myself, so I decided I must have been mistaken."

Many GCoAs struggle in treatment with their resistance to admitting there was something wrong. They also have difficulty believing that it was "that bad" when they compare their lives with ACoAs who had more visible trauma. When they do share openly, they feel a great deal of guilt and question whether they are exaggerating and misrepresenting how it was. Many who are in recovery, report overcoming this guilt with help and in time.

9. Shame For Being Chemically Dependent

Grandchildren who are recovering from chemical dependency (34% of those surveyed) experience extreme shame for bringing the disease back into the family (65% of the recovering people identified this as an issue). In many ways they feel worse for what it (their addiction) has done to their parents than what it did to them personally.

One stated, "Along with my low self-esteem and self-loathing, I could not even keep a low profile and become invisible as I wanted to do so badly. I felt I was a shame, a contaminator in the family".

Many have never told their families of their recovery and carry this secret for fear of their family's reaction.

One who involved her mother said, "When I went into treatment, my mother said to me 'We can take care of this in the family, don't go'. Thank God, in my illness, I could be honest enough to know that was impossible!"

In addition to dealing with the fear of family rejection, GCoAs have difficulty accepting alcoholism as a disease. Without a visible alcoholic parent, they believe they have brought this on themselves. In addition to the sense of moral failure often accompanying this disease, the GCoA carries the burden of bringing alcoholism back into the family after it has skipped a generation. They also may feel the burden of guilt for making their parents "look bad" or inadequate as parents.

Discovering an alcoholic grandparent often provides relief from the self-blaming and acceptance of their powerlessness over the disease. Without the moralism and judgments of themselves as bad people, their chances for long-term sobriety are improved and they are more able to use AA with a sense of belonging, believing they have a right to be there.

The information gathered to compile this list of characteristics of Grandchildren of Alcoholics is by no means complete. Since it may be the first time these questions have been asked, it is my hope that it will stimulate interest in more thorough research of a more scientific nature.

Problem Areas In The Adult
Lives Of Grandchildren

When questioned about areas of difficulty in their present lives, Grandchildren strongly resemble Adult Children of Alcoholics. However, one major difference may be that they did not know that these problems were related to the presence of alcoholism in the family. Many Grandchildren assumed that this was just the way "people" were and there was nothing unusual about it. For the most part, GCoAs had no trouble identifying the issues they are struggling with today. These are the major problem areas for Grandchildren:

1. Difficulty With Relationships — 63% Identified

Most GCoAs reported general problems with maintaining healthy relationships. The issues of intimacy, trust and identity are problem areas for Grandchildren. Also reported were frequent relationships with chemically dependent persons, i.e., spouses, children and lovers. Grandchildren, who have had little or no modeling for healthy communication, sharing feelings, negotiating, decision-making within an intimate relationship, attempt to duplicate the external appearance of health and do not experience the positive outcome they seek.

Like their ACoA parents, they expect an intimate relationship to give them self-worth and a feeling of security. They tend to pair up with individuals who have a common history and are also looking for things a relationship cannot really provide. In this case, two halves do not make a whole, and the GCoA is left believing that they must try harder, and begin the effort to control and change the other person, or that they themselves are not capable of intimacy and give up entirely.

2. Out of Touch with Feelings — 55% Identified

Many grew up in family systems where they were rarely, if ever, asked "How do you feel?" Many instead report hearing more often, "*Don't* feel that way!" Again, modeling was not present; the language of feelings was not taught. The outcome for Grandchildren was that they learn to mimic feelings or simply disclaim them.

Among persons who struggle with this issue, there are several variations. Some report feeling very little, a numbness and inability to experience even the physiological sensations associated with feeling. In many respects they have lost, through atrophy, their ability to react to the stimuli around them.

Others report having the physical responses: butterflies in the stomach, sweaty palms, blotchy neck, blushing, etc., but do not have the language to describe their feelings nor the ability to distinguish one from another.

The GCoA who is out of touch with feelings may be unable to have intimacy until he/she begins to identify her/his feelings.

3. Poor Self-Worth — 59% Identified

The low self-worth of GCoAs may at times be better disguised than their ACoA counterparts. They have learned how to look okay even when they don't believe it themselves. Without appropriate help, they go around in circles adjusting and re-adjusting their "outsides" to be more acceptable to the world, only to find that with their first mistake, they fall apart. Feelings of inadequacy and self-blame prevail with the added shame that "I should be okay. There is no reason for me to feel like this, therefore, it's wrong." When poor self-worth is not acknowledged, it becomes a big secret which must be kept at all costs. Thus the cycle of trying harder to look okay. One outward sign of low self-worth for GCoAs may be a defensive posture, even when it is inappropriate or unnecessary. They have difficulty admitting any personal or family fault, and may overly defend unimportant issues. This "protesting too much" is a sure sign of the inner conflict.

"If you find out that I have a fault, you won't want any of me" (i.e., total abandonment). This fear is a direct result of living with the conditional love of low self-worth parents.

4. Feel Angry a Lot — 43% Identified

This area is one of major concern to ACoAs in treatment and is a serious problem area for Grandchildren as well. They consistently report not being permitted to express anger, and yet watched one or both parents express rage regularly. Many are able to contain the anger while in the family setting but begin to "ooze" inappropriately when they begin an independent adult lifestyle.

Rage is not an everyday response to a healthy person. Anger stays at the level of irritation and annoyance unless a major tragic event occurs to stir up rage. GCoAs have developed an ability to discount minor annoyances until the "last straw" causes them to blow up without cause or explanation, possibly doing serious harm to their interpersonal relationships or jeopardizing their jobs. The anger they are expressing is not over the minor incident at hand, but over the years of being a "victim" who was not allowed to express anger without increasing problems at home.

They may also be unconsciously carrying the unexpressed anger of their parents who were trying so hard to look good. These parents may have viewed any expression of anger as a sign of dysfunction, believing that happy couples and families don't fight. What parents don't deal with from their past, their children inherit and play out in their lives.

The negative consequences of feeling angry range from strained relationships, to ulcers, to child abuse. GCoAs feel helpless to relieve this inner "burning" and need a safe setting in which to effectively discharge anger from the past. This process will be explained in more detail in Chapter 5.

SUMMARY

GCoA Family Patterns

- Most Grandchildren of Alcoholics were never told about their grandparent's alcoholism.
- Their ACoA parents did not acknowledge the negative effects of living with alcoholism.
- Addictions other than chemicals were present, especially work and food.
- Most Grandchildren were repeatedly told they had a *Good Family*.
- A small number of GCoAs feel the love their parents attempt to express.

Characteristics of Grandchildren of Alcoholics

In addition to the standard lists of ACoA characteristics, Grandchildren identify:

1. Distorted family image — seeing only the good in their families.
2. Self-blaming.
3. Good at forming superficial relationships — struggle with intimacy.
4. Difficulty asking for help.
5. Struggle with compulsive behaviors.
6. Tend to be secretive.

7. Prone to episodes of depression and anxiety.
8. Strong family loyalty.
9. Shame for becoming chemically dependent.

Major Problem Areas Reported By GCoAS In Adult Life

• Difficulty with relationships.
• Out of touch with feelings.
• Poor self-worth.
• Feeling angry a lot.

_____Chapter 4_____

The Subtle Abuses In Co-dependent And Chemically Dependent Families

Where there is chemical dependency and/or co-dependency, there is abuse. 90% of those seeking treatment for co-dependency report being abused in some way. Half report physical and/or sexual abuse, half identify with being verbally abused. The other 10% are frequently victims as well, but either do not remember or have a distorted sense of what is abusive. With education and treatment they, too, identify as victims.

In my work with Adult Children of Alcoholics I have heard the painful stories of adults who were severely abused as children, victims of physical and emotional abuse beyond belief. Those who experienced the extremes of verbal, sexual and/or physical abuse are very conscious of its damaging effects on their lives. Most of us would agree that this type of abuse leaves lifetime scars on its victims. As I listen painfully to their stories of beatings, threats of murder, abandonment, deprivation and severe neglect, I have been acutely aware of their distorted sense of what they should expect in relationships, as to what is "normal".

They express gratitude in their adult lives for those who do not beat them, rape, steal, etc., and have minimal expectations of those they interact with on a daily basis other than "Don't hit me". I am particularly struck by the "abuses" they do not see in the past or present, focusing only on the extremes and believing that they would be content with a life free of physical, sexual or verbal abuse.

Society has contributed to this tendency to recognize and treat only the extreme cases, the "late stage victim" if you will, ignoring the abuses we inflict upon each other in our daily interactions. Who among us has not been abused at least once by an angry doctor, waitress, bus-driver, policeman or mother-in-law? We have come to accept these occasional encounters as the norm since we cannot do anything about them. Our world is filled with angry people who will vent their feelings on any available target. Fortunately, most of these people are not vital to our self-esteem and we are relatively unaffected. More serious, however, is the emotional abuse we inflict and suffer within our intimate relationships.

Grandchildren of Alcoholics are frequently victims of emotional abuse and cannot report any of the extreme examples given by Adult Children of Alcoholics. The damage done, in terms of impact on adult functioning, is very similar regardless of how dramatic or subtle the abuse in their childhood.

It is my belief that both Adult Children and Grandchildren and, of course, anyone from a dysfunctional home suffer from emotional abuse. Despite the fact that this abuse is generally unidentified, (because it isn't "that bad"), it is deeply damaging to self-esteem and creates a cycle of victimization for life. Our spirits are not as resilient as our bodies. Where abuse is invisible, victims internalize the pain and blame themselves.

Whether the Adult Child who has visible trauma in the past, or the Grandchild whose emotional needs were neglected, the outcome is a victim lifestyle. The severity of abuse (e.g., incest) will naturally determine how seriously a person is damaged and will set the time necessary for recovery, but the outward extreme abuse is not necessarily the only issue facing the victim. Full recovery requires development of a keen sense of when something doesn't feel right and preventing the re-occurrence of victimization.

Redefining Abuse

My definition of abuse is any behavior which deliber-atly, or even inadvertently, damages or detracts from the self-esteem of any human being. The readers' immediate reaction might be that according to this definition, almost any action can be interpreted as abuse. I am not suggesting that everytime a waitress forgets the cream for your coffee she is abusing you. How we internalize these everyday occurrences is going to determine to some degree how much our self-esteem will be affected.

Several variables may influence how significantly we are affected:

The Importance We Place
On The Relationship Involved

If we value and desire the approval of another person and do not receive their acceptance, in fact are mistreated or ignored by them, the abuse will be very painful and possibly damaging.

Example: If a co-worker whom I barely know does not acknowledge my presence when I arrive at work in the morning, I may not even notice. If my best friend does the same thing when we meet on the street, I am deeply affected, at least temporarily.

Role Expectations

By definition of society certain roles imply certain behaviors. A parent is expected to be attentive to the physical and emotional needs of a child. Parents are are aware of this expectation. A husband or wife is generally expected to show concern about the emotional and/or physical well-being of their spouse. A boss is expected to be respectful in the use of authority. It is natural to have these types of expectations in our significant relationships. When a person, particularly if they are in a role of authority, violates the boundaries of that role and does not hold up their end of the emotional contract involved, the impact on the victim can be devastating.

Although occasionally our expectations can be irrational and unfair, those I am referring to here are part of an unspoken agreement between spouses, parent and child, boss and employee, teacher and student, etc. When there are no expectations of à particular role, there is less likely to be a painful reaction.

Example: Many spouses of alcoholics were married with the expectation that when children came along, they would be the shared responsibility of both parents. When the opposite occurs, deep disappointment and disillusionment result. If this expectation were not part of their "contract", it would not be as painful.

Our Emotional State At The Time Of The Incident

Our reaction to an abusive incident, even when the relationship is not a significant one, can depend a great deal on the feelings we are having at the time.

Example: If my husband decides to discuss his need for space at a moment when I am feeling particularly vulnerable or exhausted, I will experience this as rejection and possibly call it abusive. Perhaps at a different moment I would be able to listen and negotiate with little emotional reaction, recognizing this as his right to express himself honestly.

Age

Children are most often helpless victims to the abuses inflicted by their parents. They do not have the option of leaving, and expressing themselves honestly may only increase the abuse. The emotional abuse that occurs before the age of five may not even be remembered by a child but may be the most damaging in terms of impact on their future relationships.

Example: A three year old whose father becomes extremely critical after a drinking episode cannot connect the behavior to the drinking, and will simply accept that this is the way Daddy is sometimes. The damage is done regardless of why Daddy does it. A twelve year old may be able to partially attribute Daddy's change in behavior to his drinking, and not totally personalize the criticism. Both are hurt by the abuse, but age and ability to reason may ease the severity.

Prior Experiences With Abuse

Victims of abuse will often have a history of years of abuse by parents, siblings, intimate partners, friends, employers, even their own children. The history of abuse within a particular relationship will influence the reaction to the present abuse. If you have done it to me dozens of times before, the hurt will be deep and may be unforgivable. If this is the first time, it may be discounted and forgotten.

A person who was abused as a child will suffer from the cumulative effect of the abuse each time it occurs in their adult relationships. Whether or not they acknowledge or even remember the past abuses, the damage has left open wounds which are painfully exposed with each incident. Repression may allow victims to block out the memory and deny the pain, but the intensity of the experience is relived with each recurrent abuse.

Level of Self-Esteem

Persons with high self-worth are abused less often than those with low self-worth. At the same time when they have good feelings about themselves, they are more able to avoid abusive people and situations and to cope with them when they do occur without internal devastation.

Somehow they know they are okay, even though they may be hurt. It is only when the abuse continues that self-worth is diminished significantly. The same painful event can happen to two people with different levels of self-worth and be perceived very differently by each.

Example: An ACoA has a teenage son who has decided that he wants to spend the July Fourth holiday at his girlfriend's home. With low self-worth the parent perceives this as "You don't love me. You think her mom is nicer. You are ungrateful and abusive." The high self-worth mother reacts instead with "I'm disappointed that you won't be with us but you are growing up and need to make your own decisions." Abuse is then in the "eye of the beholder".

Support System

It is amazing to see individuals and families recover from trauma and tragedy with relative ease when they have a strong support system behind them. This support may be family, friends, spiritual, religious or 12-step support groups, etc., but if it is accepting and consistently available, it can make a huge difference in how an individual views his reality.

When we know that there are a group of people who approve of us, maybe even agree with our position on things, we can take risks and survive the bumps and bruises of relationships with minimal pain and scarring. Abuse feels much more abusive when we are in it alone. The disheartening fact is, however, that victims, particularly from alcoholic families, are not in the habit of forming support systems or asking for help of any kind. The very people who need it most have it least.

When a person who is isolated in a dysfunctional family system experiences even minor abuses, they feel like major crises.

Example: A GCoA receives a number of critical comments on her performance evaluation at work. She feels they were unjustified and suffers a major depression for weeks, contemplating quitting her job. She feels abused and unappreciated. An alcoholic in recovery in AA has a similar experience, goes to his sponsor or a meeting to discuss it and views this as an opportunity to grow and perhaps improve his job performance. With the aid of a healthy support system, individuals in recovery will find that much of what they once perceived as abusive is *No Big Deal!*

When viewing this list of variables in the context of co-dependency, it is clear that Children and Grandchildren of Alcoholics would not only be abused more frequently due to the presence of the disease, but its impact would be more devastating because of the conditions surrounding them.

What feels abusive to one person may be meaningless to another. The extreme abuses are much easier to label since society has determined that physical abuse, incest and extreme verbal abuse are not acceptable behaviors. The impact of emotional abuse is much more personal and subtle. More important than evaluating each incident is the cumulative effect and the resulting pattern of a victim lifestyle, which creates the climate and opportunity for further abuse. Unless a victim knows that he or she is a victim, the pattern cannot be avoided.

The following are examples of emotional abuse which may go unnoticed even by professionals but over time will severely damage a person's self-esteem.

As young children, victims may have lived with:

- Harsh controlling discipline, enforced through humiliating, belittling, sarcasm, teasing, name-calling, constant monitoring and criticism.
- No discipline or limits. Children must decide for themselves about right and wrong, safe and unsafe.
- Rigid parenting. There is a *RIGHT* way to do everything. Very tight limits and excessive rules prevent children from learning to express their individuality or learning to make any choices in life.
- Silent violence. Not talking for long periods of time is used to control and punish. Parents withdraw from each other and their children saying non-verbally "I don't love you anymore."
- Moodiness and inconsistency. Whether chemically induced or not, children are forced to anticipate and adapt to frequent mood swings of parents, who are sometimes elated and sometimes depressed without warning.
- Parents airing their difficulties with their spouse in front of or even directly to their children. Com-

plaints about the behavior, drinking, frequent absences or even sexual concerns are discussed openly within hearing range of children, without regard for how this may hurt them.

- Dependence on children for moral support, asking their advice on adult problems, treating a child as a friend, confidante or even spouse. A mother may comment, "I don't know what I'd do without my daughter, she's my best friend. We're so close, I can tell her anything."

- Passivity or weakness on the part of a parent who watches children being hurt or abused and does nothing about it. This parent is often seen as the innocent victim, "good guy", in the family. Children do not feel protected or even supported and do not want to burden the good parent further.

- Feelings are not permitted to be expressed openly. Crying is something children do infrequently and alone. Anger may only be okay for parents but is punishable for children. Fear is something you hide and shouldn't feel.

- Neglect of the emotional pain, hurts, etc., of children. When a child looks sad or down, it is a parent's responsibility to notice and ask "What's wrong?" Some children are expected to ask for what they need before they are capable of doing it. Children are allowed to isolate themselves, in fact, are praised for not being a bother to parents.

- Threats of beatings, abandonment or other severe punishment which may never materialize but control children through fear and terror of what might happen if they don't comply. Some children have witnessed siblings being beaten and are controlled by the memories.

- Lack of affection and touch. Some children are touched as infants but have no memory of affection beyond that age.

- Play, laughter and spontaneity are not permitted and

have to be done secretly or outside of the home. Children are not allowed to be children but are expected to be "little adults". The message is "Hurry up and grow up; we don't like children."

- Age-inappropriate parenting. Parents who either expect too much of young children in terms of limits and responsibilities, or overly restrict older children, preventing them from growing up and leaving.
- Smothering and over-protection. To a child this feels like "My mother needs me more than I need her. I better stay close."
- Uneven or inconsistent parenting, obviously favoring one child and constantly criticizing or outwardly abusing another. The favored child is as abused emotionally as the outwardly abused one.

As adults, victims may continue to be abused and live with:

- Extremely dependent relationships with friends, spouses, relatives. They are in "lopsided" relationships where their role is to be available, take care of and support, rarely getting anything in return.
- Telephone abuse. Victims may be harrassed on the telephone by those who depend on them, calling at all hours of the day or night with their problems, needs or demands. They may also take every opportunity to criticize and put them down. Victims do not realize they have the option of hanging up and don't want to hurt the feelings of the abusive person. Their motto is "If someone's feelings must be hurt, it might as well be mine."
- Affairs or continual flirting on the part of spouses or partners. Some may listen to a spouse talk about how attractive others are but not act on it.
- Forced sex accomplished with emotional blackmail, rather than physical abuse. The abuser is making it clear that "Life with me will be miserable if you

don't give in to my desires". There may be a total lack of regard for the feelings, or even physical discomfort, of the victim who is called "frigid" for not enjoying it.

- Withholding sex in intimate relationships as a means of expressing rage and maintaining control.
- Irrational mood swings and "Jekyll and Hyde" personalities in loved ones, which the victim is expected to accommodate, prevent, cover up, etc.
- Financial abuses:

  Living with a spouse or partner who refuses to work or contribute to household expenses when this support was previously agreed upon. They may lose jobs frequently or simply have trouble finding work for long periods of time.

  Control through financial deprivation. The primary wage-earner may keep tight control on money, giving none or minimal amounts to their spouse and family. Income is a well-kept secret.

  Compulsive spending, credit card addiction and compulsive gambling lead to continual financial and emotional unmanageability identical to that of chemical dependency. There are many victims including the addict.

- Unavailability and irresponsibility in a spouse. Although it is not anticipated, many adults find themselves with an extra child who requires limits, directions and parenting — in their spouse. Not only do they not help or support, but they demand and depend as much as a child and expect that someone will enable them.
- Abuse by their own children. When no clear limits have been set for children, they will respond with demands, verbally and perhaps even physically, until limits are set. Many adults must contend with the consequences of weak discipline when their children are adolescents and have little or no respect for authority. Parents may be

totally out of control and serve as "doormats" to their children.

- Abuse in the workplace. Victims are found on the job as well as at home. They may experience sexual harrassment, undue stress, demands and pressures, etc., and feel incapable of setting any limits. They may spend 40 hours per week in painfully uncomfortable working conditions with people who verbally abuse and overly depend on them. Victims may be easily "conned" and manipulated by bosses and co-workers and be easy prey for abusers. They are convinced they should be grateful for the job and must put up with some abuse to keep it.

While reviewing the list of "adult abuses", it is clear that there is no such thing as a completely helpless victim. Very seldom, as adults, are we totally without options. Keep in mind, however, who the victim really is and what their life experience has been.

If they come from a family system where they watched their parents be abused, and were then abused by their parents, do they really have any choice? Without the model of healthy choicemaking and limit-setting, the victim has no norm by which to measure his or her present circumstances. Particularly in regard to the more subtle everyday abuses, they see nothing extreme about it, and are not about to risk making things worse by confronting and "rocking the boat". They react with "It could be worse, at least I have a husband . . . at least he doesn't hit me . . ." It's better than it was when I was a kid . . . " Once informed, and treated, Adult Children and Grandchildren of Alcoholics can begin to make choices and are increasingly more responsible for the quality of their lives, but until then, they live a familiar victim lifestyle.

The Victim Lifestyle

Victims frequently ask the question "Why me?" Frustrated with the continuous pattern of abusive situations in which they find themselves, they conclude that God is out to destroy them or they are just not meant to be happy. Knowledge of the feelings and behaviors which set them up for victimization can begin to break the cycle. There are definite indicators that a person is in a victim lifestyle:

1. An Inability To Set Limits or Boundaries In Most Areas of Their Lives

To begin with, victims have not developed enough identity to know what they want, like, believe, feel. They are therefore at a strong disadvantage in any relationship where the other person does know these things. The fact is if you don't have a preference or can't make a choice, in most situations, someone will be glad to make it for you.

This problem becomes a general one for victims, affecting their marriages, parenting, friendships and work relationships. The word "NO" is foreign to them. They wait for the people around them to stop demanding things or they will try to hint at their frustration. They will frequently make statements like "When is it my turn? Nobody appreciates me!" instead of saying "I don't want to do that favor for you today."

Even on rare occasions when a victim does know what they want, they don't know how to communicate it.

For example: Joanne feels neglected by her husband and would like to go to a movie or dinner with him. She says, "Joe is taking Sue to the movies again. We never go anywhere!" Joanne believes she has expressed her need and is disappointed when she doesn't get results. She then says to Sue, "It's no use, I ask and he won't listen."

Victims believe they are being clear and direct. When asked a question like, "Did you tell your friend how you feel about being taken advantage of?" they answer, "He knows how I feel!"

A true victim sees a telephone as the enemy. It may control their lives because every time it rings, they have a duty and an obligation to hold the receiver to their ear until the other party is satisfied that the conversation is over. This call may be at 5 p.m. while you are preparing dinner, with a crying three-year-old on one leg and a 10-year-old asking for help with homework while the "friend" at the other end has had a bad day at work and wants you to listen.

I once asked a 27-year-old Adult Child to list to her group all of the people she felt responsible for on a regular basis. Her answer was:

— Her recovering alcoholic husband who did not go to AA and relied on her to support him emotionally.
— Her three children, ages 3, 5 and 6.
— Her drunk mother-in-law who called daily to criticize the way she ran her home.
— The church choir where she sang and practiced two nights and Sundays every week.
— Her AA group and the two women she sponsored.
— Her active alcoholic sister who lived nearby and called to cry several times a week about her marriage.
— A weekly church group where she was required to pray silently in church several hours doing "Perpetual Adorations."

The idea that she could change this by learning to set limits was a totally foreign concept. She had no idea how impossible a situation she had placed herself in. With help she realized that she needed to put her energy where it really mattered.

The issue of boundaries is a difficult one for victims. Boundary setting is something most people learn without any conscious awareness. Our parents and other adults model appropriate boundaries and teach and honor our boundaries. Their response to a child's need for space and loving touch gives him or her the cues they will rely on in later years to determine the rightness of their contacts with others. In chemical and co-dependent families, parents may themselves be victims and have no sense of their own boundaries.

When Uncle Harry hugs 12-year-old Susan too long, Mom (who is ACoA) says nothing. When Susan complains, she is told it is her imagination and she should never say things like that about him. She is told not to trust her own instincts. Over time Susan loses that instinct.

Sexual abuse is rarely an isolated incident. When a person has been violated as a child, and discounted when they report it, they lose their ability to sense when something is not okay. As a result they may be victim to repeated sexual abuse. It starts out with Dad or Uncle Harry, then her brother, his friends, her doctor, therapist, etc. Unfortunately, victims blame themselves for being seductive or evil and inviting it. I do not believe it is invited. The problem is that they do not see it coming until it is too late to prevent, and then they do not have the tools or strength to fight it off.

2. Fear Is The Dominant Emotion

Fear of the reaction or behavior of other people is the primary motivator for a victim. They make whatever choice or decision will cause the least amount of waves. They are unable to ask themselves what they would like to do, what movie they enjoy, what they want for dinner, etc., but will be "hypervigilant" to the wants and needs of others. They have an instinctive ability to assess the feelings and desires of significant people, within seconds if necessary, to make a choice that may be more popular.

Ironically, the more they try to please others, the more they upset them. It is impossible to please everyone at the same time and when my mother is happy with me, my husband is not. The fear is of disapproval, anger, even violence or abandonment. Persons who have been accustomed to conditional love, focus their energy on earning love and approval by doing what others want.

Victims rarely relax and enjoy the moment they are in because they are acutely aware of where they "should" be or worry about the person who might be waiting for them. No one should be inconvenienced or burdened, except the victim, of course. They live in anticipation of the negative response of others, having adapted for years to the mood swings and "Jekyll and Hyde" personalities of family members.

This fear makes the victim an easy target for manipulation since anyone wishing to dominate or impose their will, will undoubtedly win if they can intimidate or threaten with verbal abuse. The fragile low self-esteem of the victim cannot withstand the battering of a simple disagreement and even when they believe they are right, they eventually give in.

The fear progressively increases, particularly in those who have been victims since childhood, and may turn into paralyzing anxiety or worry about what is ahead. The victim becomes unable to make any decision for fear of making the wrong one.

Well-meaning professionals are often baffled by the inability of victims to make decisions, even when their survival or that of their children depend on it. The fear of being alone can be the most powerful fear of all, keeping victims in abusive situations with the belief that they could not survive without the abusive person.

3. Compulsive Need For Intimacy

I once worked in a home for adolescent girls who were from homes where their physical needs, as well as emotional needs, were not met. They were forced to steal to get enough to eat and many had lived on the street for some time in hunger. When they were institutionalized, they were given more than adequate amounts of food at every meal with large snacks available in between meals. Despite the availability of food, it was not uncommon to find the girls stealing food, hiding it in their bedrooms only to see it spoil, all for fear of not getting enough.

This is the way it is emotionally for victims of abuse. They have lived with, at best, inconsistent nurturing and although they have no idea what intimacy is, they know they don't have it and seek it at every opportunity. One person describes it as having a "hole in their gut with the wind blowing through". A great deal of energy is used trying to fill up the emptiness but unfortunately victims tend to be "Looking for love in all the wrong places."

In their compulsive search for intimacy, victims sometimes mistake infatuation or chemistry for the real thing. It feels wonderful to be touched, wanted and, to a degree, cared for. They center their whole lives around this new and exciting person who three months later turns into a frog. Rather than say, "You are a frog", the victim says, "If I wait long enough or kiss well enough, he will become a prince." And so they wait and try to turn this person into the man or woman of their dreams. At the same time they abandon all other supports, friends, interests, etc., to dedicate all of their energy into re-creating that wonderful feeling they had in the beginning.

If by a strange fluke, a victim happens to find a reasonably healthy person who is capable of intimacy, they take this person hostage, and may destroy the relationship with possessiveness and insecurity. Because of their low self-esteem when they find a good thing, they don't believe they deserve it and never trust that it is really there. Jealousy may be overwhelming and the victim may drive their partner away with unfounded suspicion and accusations.

Another variation is the victim who has experienced enough of the above difficulties and decides that it is too painful and it is better to be alone — forever, if necessary.

Victims may behave similarly in their friendships, expecting constant availability, unending loyalty, total honesty and exclusivity before they can feel intimate and safe. Without a realistic idea of what intimacy is, victims will rarely find it. They have not experienced the normal developmental stages of relating intimately within the family, with same-sex friends, opposite-sex friends, dating and finally romantic intimacy.

4. Under-reactors and Over-reactors

Victims have learned to repress pain and overlook major abuses in their lives. Many live with the list of abuses earlier described and do not acknowledge that any of them are a problem. They under-react to things some of us observe with shock and horror.

Victims in some ways live one day at a time, one incident at a time, never looking at the situation and noticing that they are often in the same messes over and over, or that there is the same pattern of abuse in their relationships. They live from crisis to crisis, maybe even enraged or deeply hurt, but unable to really face the seriousness of it. They become skilled at sweeping things under the rug, accepting promises that it won't happen again, thus insuring that it will.

When a victim has a moment of reality, they must face the possibility that they will have to take action, make a decision, possibly lose the relationship entirely. The paralysis of fear sets in and they quickly find a way to rationalize the abuse away. Many men and women live with spouses who for a period of years are unfaithful continuously. The victim at first may refuse to see the affairs, even denying them when others tell them the truth. Once they can no longer deny, they will rationalize that the "other woman or man" seduced my spouse, and once he/she gets it out of their system, it will end. They do not discuss it openly and refuse to face it internally. Their children may even be aware and must painfully watch as the victim denies reality. I have known this type of denial to go on for years, eventually settling in to a sick acceptance of the once unacceptable.

Where does the anger go when one is unable or unwilling to direct it to its source? Obviously, it takes its toll physically, but it will also be apparent as an over-reaction to trivia. Spilled juice or someone late for dinner can arouse intense rage that has been stored for years. Children and pets will be targets for sudden outbursts. Traffic, slow store clerks, society at large, politicians, anyone who will not hold the victim accountable will get a share.

When victims first arrive in therapy, they will present all of these details about the behavior of others as the reason for their bad feelings. The major abuse will often be a well-kept secret until a therapist or group can observe and point out the patterns to the victim. They are sincerely deluded and believe that they are not angry about, or even bothered by, the major problems.

5. Extreme Thinking

At the moment of truth, which usually occurs in the midst of crisis, the victim decides that this is the time to take action. Through the fog of rage and hurt, they plan their escape — "I'll pack up and move to Seattle." "I'll show her, I'm going to have an affair, too!" "I'll disappear and let him think I killed myself. That'll show him!" "I'll tell my boss off. I don't care about this job anyway!" "These kids don't appreciate me. I'm going to disappear!"

These and many other similarly crazy thoughts cross the minds of victims before the process of repression takes over. Some relief is gained from screaming in their heads. They may even feel as if they had taken the action, had the argument they rehearsed, quit the job. Once they have taken the edge off the anger through mental discharge, they begin to forget it ever happened. The next time they see the person involved or face a similar situation, they may feel nothing more than a twinge of discomfort.

In between crises the victim dreams about a better life, when the right person will come and make it all right. They believe that someday those who care will say "Joe, thank you for everything you've done for us over the years. We really appreciate it, but we don't need anything else. Now *It's Your Turn!*"

The extremes of positive and negative thoughts are a continuous pattern for victims. They see things as *all* good, or *all* bad. In every argument, someone is *right,* someone *wrong,* with a winner and a loser. They may go around in circles this way for years, playing back the same tapes, dealing with the same, or very similar problems over and over, never resolving anything.

6. Passivity

When all is said and done, victims do nothing. Despite a lot of noise and threats, rarely does a victim take any decisive action. When they do make a decision, it is on impulse and generally undone as quickly as it took place.

A former client who was an abused child and later married an abusive alcoholic, in fact the town drunk, was into a regular routine of leaving, moving van and all, but returning within the same weekend. Many a co-dependent has been heard on numerous occasions saying, "This is the last time".

Given a disturbing work situation, victims will find other victims to complain to in order to let off steam, but will be unable to change jobs, even when opportunities present themselves. They will complain that a therapist isn't helping them, or a serviceman is taking advantage, but will not take any action.

A contributing factor to this passivity is the secondary gain, or "pay off" for being a victim. They may arouse sympathy, and gain much needed attention through their inaction, which they do not get in their primary relationships.

As we have learned with ACoAs, victims become very accustomed to living in crisis. During the crisis, they can focus on surviving the insanity and do not have to feel the pain that comes up during the quieter moments. Being alone with oneself can be the most painful time of all. If we feel we have no other identity, problems can help to define who we are. Unfortunately, like the addict looking for new doctors to write prescriptions, the victim must find new people willing to hear the same old story for the umpteenth time.

7. Self-Blame and Guilt

Regardless of the severity of the abuse, victims to a large extent see themselves as responsible. They do not see the abuser as responsible for his/her behavior and believe that "If only I weren't there at that time. If I tried a little longer. If I didn't yell back . . ." When they view the same event objectively in someone else's life, they are able to see the powerless position they were in. But without help, they cannot see their own lack of control over the situation.

Victims are not voluntarily making informed choices to stay in unhealthy situations or relationships. Even if they were, that in no way excuses or justifies the abusive behavior of others. Just because I contributed by being angry, that does not give someone else the right to respond abusively. Victims have difficulty separating their behavior from that of the abuser, and holding the abuser accountable for his actions.

8. Physical Illness and Addiction

Very simply put, if painful feelings, especially anger, are not expressed, they take their toll in physical symptoms. Feelings don't discriminate and choose a particular way of appearing in our bodies, but they do take advantage of our weak areas, perhaps determined by heredity or even environment. We each have our areas of susceptibility, some are more likely to suffer from headaches, others from gastro-intestinal difficulties, but we will all internalize our pain one way or another if it is not expressed.

Common to victims are many stress-related illnesses, e.g., migraines, colitis, allergies, ulcers, chronic back pain, aggravated rheumatoid arthritis. Less often identified are sleep and eating disturbances, eating disorders, an inability to recover from normal illness, i.e. colds and flu, within reasonable time periods.

Abuse of chemicals, which may later develop into addiction, is one means of coping with a victim lifestyle. Other addictions like smoking, food, sex, gambling may appear.

A contributing factor to the physical illness is also the fact that a martyr-type victim does not, because of the nature of the assumed role, take care of her/himself.

Illness may become another means of seeking and gaining attention. Taking responsibility for oneself is not part of a victim lifestyle. In some cases, the physical problem may be the victim's only way to say to the abuser(s) "See my pain, it's real. Please stop hurting me." It may also be the only way for the victim to stop the constant caretaking activity and get some rest with a legitimate reason. They do not feel they can take a day off without a very good reason, therefore, they must get sick to do it.

9. Loss of Spirit

I used to call this characteristic "Loss of Spirituality", but I now see it as much more. It is the result of an accumulation of abuses over a long period of time, which eventually takes away our will to survive. To me spirit represents the child within each of us, the trusting, honest, spontaneous part that believes there is a purpose to our existence. I believe this is the part to which God communicates.

Persons who have been abused and have lived around abusiveness all their lives have a great deal of difficulty believing that there is goodness and hope in this world. They have often been taught, at least verbally, values like honesty, forgiveness, kindness, respect, but have never seen these things in action, unless on television. When they have tried, without tools or experience, to live by these standards, they have been hurt further.

At some point in a gradual decline, the victim begins to adjust his/her value system to survive the pain. This does not occur without guilt and shame. They may then fluctuate between "God is punishing me, because I'm bad" and "God is good but I'm not worthy of His love." Once a sense of hopelessness occurs, the risk of severe depression and suicide are ever present.

10. Victims Become Abusers

Every abuser is also a victim. Victims cannot survive without to some degree becoming abusive to others. No one in an abusive chemically dependent or codependent family is an innocent bystander. Even children will show signs of abusive behavior to younger siblings, friends and pets. Many adults have memories of being a "bully" to other children and live with the guilt of having abused others.

One of the blocks to recovery for parents is that they focus on the fact that they abused their children and are reluctant to look back on their own childhood pain. In a dysfunctional family system every one is hurting, whether the abuser or the victim. There are no Good Guys and Bad Guys. Recovery for victims begins with a willingness to face the ways in which they were hurt before they face their guilt and shame for hurting others.

The Way Out Of A Victim Lifestyle

Intellectual recovery is an "easier, softer way", whereby victims try to understand the abuser, themselves and the disease. They may read all available literature on the subject, discuss motives and childhood experiences in therapy groups and reach the conclusion, accurately enough, that it was no one's fault. After months or even years of this study and discussion and insight into the problem, they discover two things

1. "I'm still a victim today."
2. "I hurt."

Figuring out what was wrong is an important part of the process but not the end of the process. What happens to all the pain when a person realizes their abuser couldn't help it? Abuse is "felt" and damaging, regardless of the reasons or responsibility of the abuser. The victim continues to live the consequences until they are treated for the hurts they are carrying. I view recovery from abuse as a three-step process which requires professional intervention, a strong support system and major changes in lifestyle.

The first step in the process is to *identify* the abuse. This is happening for some of you as you read this book. Others will learn about their own history through the stories of others at 12-step meetings. Many professionals have discovered the abuse in their pasts while they were being "trained" to help others. Regardless of the door you enter, the first realization can be a very painful one.

During the identification of the abuse, the veil of secrecy is lifted and the victim admits, "It was bad; it hurt me; I've been cheated out of a childhood. I didn't deserve to be treated that way."

Memories may begin to flood in, although not always. Some people remain blocked for some time, but are aware that since they are so clearly a victim today it must be related to their past. In the absence of memories of specific abuses, victims may need to start with the present and work back over time. When we are ready to remember, we do. At this point it is not unusual to choose one parent or an ex-spouse to be angry with. Rarely does it all become clear at once. Identifying abuse is not an event and our focus of anger, or even blame, may shift frequently through the process. The important thing is that the victim faces the reality that something was wrong.

For Grandchildren of Alcoholics this may be the most difficult step of all. The delusion, secrets, loyalties in the family prevent the GCoA from seeing or admitting that there was abuse. They may need to focus on the evidence in their lives today in order to "get honest" about their past. IT IS IMPOSSIBLE TO BECOME A VICTIM WITHOUT ADEQUATE TRAINING AS A CHILD.

The second step, very soon after identifying the abuse, is to *express* the feelings related to the abuse as they come to the surface. This is where professional intervention is necessary. In a safe place with a trusted therapist and/or group (not with one's relatives), a victim can express the anger openly. It will not need to be forced or pulled out; most victims carry their anger very close to the surface. Beneath the anger is deep grief for the multitude of losses experienced over a lifetime. As feelings surface, they need to be allowed to be heard but not seen as a magical event, a cure-all in themselves. If feelings are unexpressed, the individuals will feel "stuck" and find themselves repeating the same patterns over and over, despite all the insight they have acquired.

Expressing the anger directly to the abuser may be extremely destructive in the long run. Although in a therapy setting when both parties are supported and equally equipped with tools to handle it, this may be very healing. It rarely works in any other setting. A therapy group can provide a healthier opportunity to let go without the negative consequences.

Once they have discharged rage and grief, at least to some degree, individuals will feel freer to try out new ways of relating. This does not mean they will not feel these things again, but they will probably not feel the rage with the same intensity they had initially, and after a time will experience normal ranges of anger, annoyance and irritation, rather than rage.

I believe grieving is a much more gradual process which, although helped by the initial therapeutic discharge, takes many years of tears at vulnerable times, anniversaries, places which hold reminders, sad movies, seeing little children hurt, etc. As healthy adults we seem to be able to use these opportunities to do our grieving and will feel it dissipate over the years. Feelings which may have been exploding in the past become something the recovering person has some power to control. They learn to choose the right time and the right place to express them.

The final step in the process of leaving a victim lifestyle is the one many people want to accomplish first — *understanding*. Once the first two steps are experienced, the understanding comes fairly easily. It requires no research or study of the dynamics of the disease, just an emotional acceptance of others and oneself as equally victims.

The serenity and peace, which were previously so elusive, are now attainable with surrender, instead of grim resolution and will power. Negotiating, limit-setting, "housecleaning" must be accomplished in intimate relationships. Former victims can begin to teach people how to treat them. Exuding self-esteem, they will attract those who respect that quality and have similar levels of self-esteem.

SUMMARY

In family systems where abuse has occurred, members develop a "victim lifestyle". Many people have been victims of more subtle abuses as children and are in a sense "set up" to repeat this pattern in their adult lives. Indicators of a victim lifestyle include:

- Inability to set limits and boundaries
- Fear as a dominant emotion
- Compulsive need for intimacy
- Under and over-reacting
- Extreme thinking
- Passivity
- Self-blame and guilt
- Physical illness and addiction
- Loss of spirit
- Victims become abusers

The way out is a 3-step process of identifying the abuse, expressing the pain and finally understanding and letting go.

_____Chapter 5_____

Treatment Options And Self-help For Adult Children And Grandchildren of Alcoholics

The information contained in this chapter is clearly biased by the writer's professional and personal experience. There is no "best place" or correct way to be treated for co-dependency. We have learned a great deal over the years and any experienced therapist will have their own way of doing things. The important thing is that we have gained a good sense of what does *not* work, and there are now many options available, depending upon the needs of the individual.

Seeking treatment unfortunately is not the first thing a co-dependent thinks of when they identify the problem.

They will often try "recovery through education" before accepting their need for professional assistance. Our outreach efforts to this point have been largely through word of mouth, which although very effective, do not always give accurate information or appropriate referrals. Adult Children who have received treatment are frequently very grateful, each sending back five of their friends.

Because this method of referral is so emotionally charged, it is essential that programs, facilities and private therapists not only know what they are doing, but accurately represent this to the consumer. Hopefully this is happening in most areas, but one word of caution: Many therapists are just beginning to work with Adult Children, and may not even know that a Grandchild needs help. In addition, the services offered are not always labeled in a manner that tells the client what the primary goal is, for example, education vs. treatment. This chapter is intended to make you an "informed consumer", one who can ask questions and find what you need.

Commonly Asked Questions About ACoA/GCoA Treatment

1. Does every Adult Child or Grandchild of an Alcoholic need treatment?

The old expression "If it works, don't fix it!" applies. Not everyone will be affected in the same way or with the same timing. I view treatment as a choice made by an individual who is experiencing pain in one or more areas of his or her life. This choice should not be made lightly. If it is to be successful in aiding one toward greater functioning, it will require a major investment of emotions, time, finances and a willingness to "walk through" the pain.

A decision to enter therapy means that one is ready to live with a certain amount of disruption of daily routine when feelings begin to surface, occasionally at inopportune moments. The first few months of therapy can be particularly stressful.

There are occasions when formal intervention is necessary, particularly with individuals whose behavior and feelings are causing severe physical, employment and family problems.

Don S., age 47, is an Adult Child who was showing signs of a co-dependent crisis on the job, with his health and at home. He was progressively becoming more short-tempered and suffered from chronic headaches which caused him to miss a great deal of work. When he did work, Don put in 10-to-12-hour days and looked exhausted. At home, Don was losing interest in his children, and his relationship with his wife was distant and angry.

Don's denial was such that he was unable to see the reality of his situation and seek help. Fortunately, his wife, also an ACoA, but in recovery, was able to see the signs and contacted the Employee Assistance person at his place of employment. She had tried unsuccessfully before this to convince Don to go to a counselor with her.

Her only alternative was to watch her husband die emotionally, possibly even physically, or seek professional help to do a formal intervention. After several weeks of preparation, and with the assistance of Don's co-workers and another friend, Don agreed to accept treatment in an inpatient co-dependency program.

His response to treatment was very positive because the intervention had been based on love and concern and Don was tired of hurting. Don was very grateful to his family for their efforts to arrest the progression of his illness.

One suggestion I often make to family members, is to do the obvious — try asking the person if they want help before going through the formal intervention process. Although a well done intervention can be a very positive experience for the family, it is emotionally taxing on all parties and may not always be necessary. Sometimes the co-dependent has not been asked directly whether they want help and offered treatment options.

A statement like "I see you are hurting. There is help available if you are interested. Here is a phone number you can call," could result in someone seeking treatment. Co-dependents, even those who are recovering alcoholics, do not know that they need special help for co-dependency or that help exists in their communities. They are often surprised to find out that someone knows what their problem is.

With the exception of individuals in extreme denial, most ACoAs, once educated, are capable of deciding for themselves whether they need and/or want treatment. Many will decide that they need it but choose to delay or avoid it all together. *They have the right to stay the way they are.* We cannot judge the quality of another person's life and assume that they must change or they are "sick". Each person must weigh the possible gains against the possible losses if treatment is initiated. It is true that the anticipated pain is usually worse than the actual experience. The following quotes of ACoAs one year after treatment reflect the realistic but positive outcomes:

"Treatment was a good place to begin to feel the reality of both today and the past. Since treatment, I've been feeling a good kind of hunger for life and at whatever odds, I've moved toward a direction to let peace and love grow in me and my family."

"I just thank God that everything was as bad as it was to get me to treatment. This past year has been the hardest one I've ever faced but because of it, those yet to come will be the best I've ever had. I am just now, at the age of 25, learning to be myself . . . And I'm much, much happier — and less, much less sad!"

"Getting treatment truly changed my life and my outlook on everything. Nothing has ever been as 'horrible' as prior to treatment. There have, of course, been times of discomfort but nothing like before. Actually Al-Anon and ACoA meetings never did anything for me until after treatment. Now I need them and Narcotics Anonymous equally."

Many can attest, after completing treatment, that it was worth it, but those who choose for themselves, knowing what they are in for, will take greater responsibility for the outcome for their treatment and benefit as a result.

2. Does ACOA treatment drag up pain, leaving the person "bleeding" without any support?

Many ACoAs fear becoming totally dysfunctional as a result of treatment and then having nowhere to go with their feelings. The negative focus: looking at character defects under a microscope, finding life problems you didn't know you had, acknowledging a painful childhood, etc., is a necessary first step. It is an important place to VISIT but not to live. ACoAs don't come into treatment because of how good things are. In order to motivate oneself toward recovery, it is necessary to take a look at "the bad news" before discovering the "good news", which is that you learned a great deal along the way, and that you made it to this point against all odds.

Effective treatment begins immediately to find the strengths of the individual, for this is the foundation upon which recovery must be built. This emphasis on the positive allows the ACoA/GCoA to face their pain with a belief in their ability to survive this process and the hope that this is taking them to a healthier level of functioning.

Follow-up study with ACoAs who have been through short-term inpatient treatment and one year of Aftercare consistently shows that this is a positive process. The statements of those completing treatment reflect the belief that although this is a painful process, they know why they are going through it, and are able to see the healing taking place. The positive qualities they were unable to "own" and accept become part of the person's identity, replacing the belief that these were merely attempts to con the world.

Most Adult Children seeking treatment are very frightened by the prospect of feeling all those years of pain and the expected "negative feedback". Most are shocked to find themselves also having feelings of joy for the first time, as they let others in, learn how to play and laugh as easily as they cry.

One of the most important concepts taught during the treatment process is that of a support system. With a group of loving, affirming, accepting people behind us, we can do just about anything. This is what makes it possible for the ACoA/GCoA to take the risks necessary for change. They know they are not alone, and that they will be supported throughout the process.

Of course, the therapist is an important part of this support, at least initially, but more essential is the peer group, those "real people" who can be trusted to be there. Therapists come and go, as do therapy groups. It is important for the individual to establish a strong network within their 12-step support groups and their family and friends. This network may be modified frequently, but will always be there.

3. Is there really treatment available? Doesn't a therapist have to be a recovering ACoA or have extensive training in ACoA issues to be effective?

I frequently hear the comment that there is no one out there qualified to treat Adult Children. Part of the problem may be a real scarcity of therapists but I suspect that the one-and-ten thinking of some co-dependents may lead to the assumption that if treatment isn't under my nose, it doesn't exist, and that all conditions must be perfect for treatment to be effective.

Good treatment does exist. Organizations like the National Association for Children of Alcoholics are working diligently to disseminate this information. Although many professionals and recovering persons in the addiction field have difficulty acknowledging it, there are excellent therapists doing quality treatment with ACoAs who have not been specifically trained in co-dependency. The follow-up, mentioned earlier, also indicates that although it is preferable that a therapist be enlightened about ACoA issues, many Adult Children and Grandchildren are finding qualified therapists and teaching them, through books, sharing of personal information, etc., the necessary concepts. The most successful therapists, as a rule, are those who never "know it all" about any issue. Their willingness to admit it is an indicator of whether they will be effective with the ACoA/GCoA.

It would be great if the day we discovered co-dependency, the services were already in place. The fact is that, as it occurred for the alcoholic in years past, *demand creates services.* There is no doubt that Adult Children are stating their need for treatment all over the United States. Professionals just beginning to catch up to this concept will take a few years to catch up to the demand.

The belief that it takes an ACoA to treat one is as inaccurate as, "It takes a drunk to treat a drunk." The well-founded fears and distrust on the part of the ACoA contribute to their reluctance to place themselves in the hands of anyone who doesn't know first-hand what they have been through. There are many professionals who "have been there" but have not been treated for their own issues.

Joan D. is a therapist working with Adult Children in her private practice. Prior to seeking ACoA treatment for herself, Joan admits she was often "bumping up against her own issues". As she tried to encourage her clients to cry or express anger in her therapy groups, she would find herself cutting them off and guiding them back to safer, more intellectual subjects which were less painful for her. Her belief that she must be healthier than the people she treats, and the constant feelings of inadequacy led Joan to treatment for herself.

The fact that a therapist has or has not shared the experience of living in an alcoholic home is not as important as their qualifications and reputation. Personal experience may be an asset, especially if the therapist has been through their own recovery process, but it is not a requirement.

Those who have been fortunate enough to discover their co-dependency at this point may find that their communities are not totally prepared for the demand for services. The good news is "You are discovering your problem before most other ACoAs and there is help somewhere." The bad news is "You may have to drive 40 to 50 miles to get it!"

My suggestion, if this is the case, is that you seek an intensive treatment weekend or inpatient program and find a qualified therapist to follow up for six months to a year. Many individuals are willing to drive very long distances for a good therapist. Instead of "cursing the darkness", find a way to get the help you need. When you are able, maybe you can contribute to making it different for others who are seeking help, through networking and educating.

A word to the newly discovered GCoA: If a therapist is reluctant to treat you because you don't have the dramatic past of an ACoA, try educating if that is possible, but don't waste your time and/or money trying to convince someone you are sick enough to be there. A really good therapist, trained in family systems, will understand what you are saying and will help you to make the connections with the past. Your present unmanageability will be evidence enough that something was wrong. They will welcome you in to groups with other co-dependents and help you to identify similarities.

When an individual decides that they would like to address and let go of a painful past in order to change the way they are functioning in the present, they are taking on a major project. Regardless of which treatment mode you choose, it is hard work. I believe it requires a commitment of at least one year to make your recovery a primary focus. This is something you would do if you moved into a new home, took on a new challenging job or had a baby. If you expect it to be hard work, limit the other challenges you take on at the same time, and allow a certain amount of your time and money for therapy, you will not feel resentful and stressed with the process.

4. How long should a recovering alcoholic or chemically dependent person be abstinent before seeking co-dependency treatment?

Approximately 60% of those seeking treatment as Adult Children and Grandchildren are recovering chemically dependent persons. They are the group most responsible for creating services through demand. They have known for some time that there is more to sobriety than just abstaining from the chemical. Most have had many years of sobriety and are in emotional pain which increases with time.

In the 5-1/2-day inpatient program which I direct, experience and follow-up have led to a policy requiring a minimum of six months abstinence and active involvement in a 12-step *recovery program*. These guidelines were developed to minimize the risk of relapse through addressing the co-dependency issues which naturally emerge during the first year of sobriety, while not jeopardizing sobriety as painful feelings arise.

Follow-up with recovering persons has shown that treating co-dependency at this point, and later on in recovery, in no way jeopardizes sobriety. In fact, it improves the quality of recovery, in some cases preventing relapse which would have ocurred without such treatment.

Larry, age 32, is a recovering alcoholic with nine months sobriety at the time of his ACoA treatment. He had completed a 28-day addiction treatment program and was closely following the aftercare plan suggested to him, including five to six AA meetings per week. He described himself as "white knuckling it" in reference to his recovery, expressing concern that he did not connect with people in AA and didn't feel comfortable calling anyone between meetings. His home life was progressively deteriorating because of his moodiness and uncontrollable anger, and he was certain his wife was not going to put up with him much longer. He was seeing a counselor who believed that Larry's painful childhood was at the root of his current problems, and referred him for inpatient treatment.

During his treatment week, Larry was able to discharge a great deal of rage related to his father's physical abuse, and also became aware of how much he viewed himself as like his father, i.e., a "bad person". Once the anger had been expressed and openly acknowledged, Larry began to connect with his group and could see the benefits of letting others help him through the process.

Although he was tearful and a bit more vulnerable leaving treatment, Larry felt less "at risk" for relapse than before he faced his anger. One year later Larry reports, "I really don't believe I would have made it to one year in AA if I hadn't had ACoA treatment. My wife has also begun treatment and things are getting better. I am truly enjoying AA meetings now and finally understand what they were trying to tell me about needing the support. I'm beginning to believe I have a right to happiness, too, not just staying dry."

As a professional, it has been my experience that the earlier we can address co-dependency, the easier it is to treat and the more teachable the individual. If co-dependency treatment is delayed, new defenses and addictions develop to cope with the pain, thus making it more difficult to find the feelings so long repressed.

Many recovering alcoholics arrive with 10-years' sobriety, but have the additional problems of compulsive overeating, sexual addiction, gambling, etc., to contend with. During the second six months of sobriety, the addict is physically healthier, but still humble enough to listen and learn new ways of living. They are not yet confident that their way is the best way.

It is also advisable to identify the ACoA/GCoA during their primary treatment for addiction, making a referral for co-dependency treatment part of their aftercare plan. The more specific the direction given to the addict at that time, the more likely it is that he/she will follow through.

For instance, a recommendation can be made and a date set for ACoA treatment six months in advance. Sometimes knowing that they will be able to get help in the near future can help the newly sober person to postpone the pain. The decision about whether to attend ACoA meetings during the first six months is an individual one, but is generally not advisable.

Exceptions to the six-month policy exist but are rare. These are clearly individuals for whom co-dependency is a direct block to sobriety. They have had quality treatment for addiction, maybe several experiences, attend AA, follow all directions and still cannot maintain sobriety. They are unable to repress their pain, even with the chemical. Often they are victims of other childhood traumas: incest, severe abuse and are haunted by these experiences. Treating their co-dependency, once they are detoxed, cannot harm them any further, and has been helpful in many cases.

What Is Treatment?

A range of comprehensive services for Adult Children has been developing very rapidly throughout the country within the last four to five years. Most are very new, learning and changing as experience is gained. As we become more knowledgeable about the recovery process, what works and what doesn't, we more clearly define the term "treatment" as it applies to co-dependency. There is no right way to do it, but it is important to view co-dependents as individuals who are in varying stages of pain and strength. Most services are designed to accommodate the majority, but provide a network of other professionals who can meet the needs of those with special problems or complications. Adult Children have given the addiction field a unique opportunity to build bridges with the Mental Health and Family Therapy professions, since they rarely present us with an uncomplicated list of problems.

Ideally, in each community a range of professional services is available to the ACoA/GCoA through treatment facilities, public agencies or private therapists.

Education

This is the starting point for most Adult Children and Grandchildren. Persons in extreme crises may get their education and therapy simultaneously, but most begin with workshops, seminars, books and whatever else is available.

A few weeks ago I spoke to a group of 300 professionals and other "lay" people who were curious about the Adult

Child movement. Although I spoke for only one hour, I could have responded to the painful comments and questions following for a whole day if time had permitted. The next morning I received eight calls for reservations for the ACoA treatment program.

Education does not make people hurt, it simply acknowledges the pain already present and gives an explanation for it. For many the reaction may be tears of relief that finally someone understands. I make it a point in every talk I give to say that I am a Grandchild of Alcoholism, and I inevitably hear from a group of grateful GCoAs afterward that no one in their personal lives has ever validated their experience.

Many therapists and facilities are discovering a hungry consumer when they publicize and conduct free educational sessions for and about Adult Children of Alcoholics. It is my hope that sessions like this will begin to be marketed to Adult Children from Dysfunctional Families or some similarly broad title. The Grandchildren and others from painful families will not be able to make the connection unless we let them know they are welcome. Even if we were to specifically identify GCoAs, we must remember that 75% of the time they don't know they are Grandchildren of Alcoholics.

It is important to include an educational component in any treatment for ACoA/GCoAs. There is an enormous leap forward that occurs when these individuals find out that alcoholism and/or co-dependency has something to do with their struggles today. They may not accept it immediately but once they do, a sense of relief and a sense of being understood and believed sets in. Self-blaming decreases and is replaced with a willingness to look further.

Although the therapy which follows may be similar to families with other types of stress or dysfunction, it is important to make the connection to chemical dependency where appropriate.

Among the information given to ACoA/GCoAs in the inital phases of treatment would be:

Chemical dependency and co-dependency: signs, symptoms, complications, progression, outcome if untreated.
ACoA/GCoA issues: characteristics, resulting life problems, survival skills.
Feelings and defenses: value of expressing feelings, defenses we use to cover feelings.
Family life: what is functional, healthy?; boundaries, roles, affection, family rules, etc.
Other addictions: gambling, food, sex . . .
Treatment resources in your community.

Many of the issues raised in an educational program would raise the curiosity and possibly the pain of the ACoA enough to motivate them to seek treatment/ therapy soon after. The education in itself need not be designed to encourage discharge of these feelings nor to provide the actual therapy.

I am often asked about the value of education which stirs up pain in the Adult Child and does not provide the answers. My response is that the ACoA/GCoA is in pain most of the time. It is only barely under the surface. In order to feel a need for treatment, they will need to see and feel this pain. It is not inflicted by the person or people conducting the workshop. This is simply the open door to an opportunity to go further.

ACoAs are not fragile. They have endured years of pain much worse than that arising at a seminar, and have methods of repression which serve them well. When they suddenly re-experience some of this pain, they may choose to get help with it or find another way to repress. Assuming we have made it clear that there are resources available, they can make a choice.

Support

Support is another level of care for those who are looking for an opportunity to talk about their experiences with others who understand. When I refer to support, I do not mean self-help, 12-step programs, which are a very special kind of support. I am referring to the somewhat didactic, professionally led groups available in many areas. This type of group may also serve as an assessment group, to determine readiness or appropriateness for treatment.

An example would be a time-limited group, for instance, 10 weeks, which would have an educational component each week. The group might be closed, the same people starting together and ending together, lasting one and one-half to two hours each week. Each session would give some information and allow for discussion. Confrontation, feedback, intense discharge of feelings would not be a part of this type of group.

This would be an excellent way to find out if you are ready to make the commitment to intensive therapy. It should not, however, be mistaken for treatment. It is also a good idea to utilize 12-step meetings at the same time for the ongoing support. (They do not end after 10 weeks and are available many times weekly.)

At this point in the process, or at the very beginning of therapy, it is essential that the co-dependent be evaluated for their own use of drugs and/or alcohol. Some ACoAs are seeking this assessment, paranoid about the possibility of being alcoholic, others are reluctant to discuss it. All co-dependents, even spouses and young children, need to be evaluated at the first possible opportunity. There will be no further growth and co-dependency treatment cannot be effective if someone is in an active addiction.

Despite the six-month rule for sobriety, many ACoAs enter treatment in denial of their addiction and are found out during the process.

Bruce was an ACoA married to a recovering alcoholic. He evaluated his use of alcohol by comparing himself to his wife, who he considered to be a "lush" during her active drinking years. He, on the other hand, went to work everyday and never slept around. His five to six drinks every evening and occasional weekend binges were negatively affecting most areas of his life and had led to bouts with bleeding ulcers. Bruce was confronted with his problem during ACoA treatment and referred directly to an inpatient addiction treatment program. His co-dependency treatment was postponed for six months, at which time he returned to address his ACoA issues.

When entering ACoA treatment, recovering chemically dependent individuals may also be asked about their use of drugs and alcohol. Occasionally an alcoholic will still be using drugs or a drug addict still drinking. It's wise to re-examine all use of medication, even over-the-counter, which could interfere with recovery.

It is highly possible that as an ACoA/GCoA you may have already made the choice to abstain, perhaps after a period of abusing chemicals in the past. This does not eliminate the need for evaluation. Once evaluated, a treatment plan can be devised to incorporate the chemical dependency and co-dependency. It may be necessary to postpone addressing the co-dependency for six months.

Therapy

The term "therapy" usually refers to any professional counseling by a person(s) trained to facilitate the recovery process. Services might include inpatient, outpatient, individual, group, couples, and/or family therapy. Each type of service has a role in the treatment process and ideally they work together for a total treatment plan for both the individual and his or her family.

Inpatient Treatment

Inpatient co-dependency treatment is a relatively new option for ACoA/GCoAs. It has distinct advantages and limitations which need to be considered when making a choice. Having worked in both outpatient and inpatient settings, I believe a combination of both works best.

In different parts of the country it is possible to find both short-term (ranging from weekends to eight days) and long-term (21 to 28 day) programs. Generally those who seek out long-term treatment are struggling with other complications, e.g., eating disorders, sexual addiction, dual-diagnosis, suicidal thoughts, severe depression or anxiety.

Judy, age 29, is a recovering alcoholic who realized after several years of sobriety that she was not recovering from the severe emotional damage of her childhood with an abusive alcoholic father. She had been a victim of incest as a child and also rape as an adult.

Judy was attending AA consistently and saw a therapist for individual counseling, but continued to be plagued with suicidal thoughts and anxiety attacks despite her efforts. Judy was referred to a 28-day inpatient program which included both medical and psychiatric evaluations.

During her treatment Judy had a psychotic episode as she faced her painful past and was evaluated as clinically depressed and in need of anti-depressant medication for a period of time. Although it has been a very slow process for Judy with strong outpatient follow-up and medical monitoring, she is beginning to feel better about herself and hopeful for her future.

Judy's circumstances are not typical for Adult Children. The trauma experienced in her life, in addition to being the child of an alcoholic, indicated that more extensive treatment was necessary.

The old expression "More is better" does not necessarily apply to treatment. There is no magic in the number of days treated. No matter how long the initial intensive treatment, there is still hard work ahead. Long-term inpatient treatment is more likely to be covered by insurance, but this alone is not reason enough to choose to spend a month in treatment.

One of the advantages to long-term treatment for those with complications is the medical/psychiatric evaluation and monitoring which is part of the treatment. Some Adult Children and Grandchildren may discover that they are in need of anti-depressants or other medication before they can fully recover. Prior to a decision to accept medication, it is wise to have the opinions of both a psychiatrist and a trusted therapist. (**A word of caution: The use of other mood-altering medications, like tranquilizers, can be very dangerous to a recovering addict and only a band-aid on the real problem for the non-addict.**)

Most short-term programs will refer for long-term treatment anyone needing this type of evaluation. Some long term programs will treat addiction and co-dependency in the same treatment groups, focusing totally on the addiction if this has not been previously addressed.

Short-term inpatient treatment is not as disruptive to one's daily life, but is limited to providing an opportunity to begin the recovery journey. Some co-dependents, already far along in the process, will use this as a means of getting new direction, rather than as a beginning. Short-term co-dependency treatment is adequate and appropriate for the majority of ACoA/GCoAs without major complications.

Jeff typifies the "average" ACoA. At 34 Jeff was as yet unmarried and had a history of superficial relationships. He was a high school history teacher but bored and unsure of his career choice. Jeff's relationship with his recovering alcoholic mother was strained, especially since her pressure and persistence resulted in his entering this inpatient ACoA program. Jeff had no other complicating factors, with the exception of a past history of heavy drug and alcohol use. Adult Children and Grandchildren similar to Jeff can be successfully treated in short term inpatient treatment with approximately one year of outpatient counseling afterward.

Regardless of length, in my experience, there are things that an inpatient program can provide which may be difficult to accomplish (although not impossible), in an outpatient setting:

Intensity — By eliminating outside distractions and interference, telephone, television, family and work responsibilities, it is possible to create greater emotional intensity, thus lowering defenses. This climate is conducive to change. The average co-dependent has a large number of responsibilities and activities to keep him or her from quietly feeling their pain. Once these activities are eliminated, the feelings begin to surface.

Privacy — The quiet and solitude of a treatment or retreat center provides the necessary opportunity for people to take risks they could not take if they suspected they might be seen or heard. Knowing they do not have to face the outside world with their tears or running eye makeup helps to give permission to feel. Being responsible only for themselves and given permission to express feelings as they occur can be a very healing experience.

Safety — Physical safety, knowing you will not be hurt by yourself, staff and/or other patients, is necessary as well. The emotional safety is something the ACoA/GCoA counts on in participating in an inpatient program. Proper screening, clear guidelines for behavior, trained staff who are willing to take charge and protect, are all a part of conveying a feeling of safety. There are occasions, although rare, when an individual loses self-control, particularly with their anger. Experienced therapists know how to diffuse the anger and protect other group members to prevent emotional or physical harm.

Emotional Discharge — Given the above conditions, it is possible to let go emotionally in an inpatient setting.

The release of rage, followed often by deep grieving, is accomplished without fear of "losing it" and not being able to function. The patient does not have to function right away and is given the healing time with the treatment group before coming back to the real world.

Community — The treatment group or "community" represents family, co-workers, friends and society. Living and working in a group of 10 or more, the patient is able to see him or herself through the eyes of others. In the intense protective environment, they will find themselves acting in the same ways that are troublesome to them in the real world. However, the feedback will be constructive and directive. Hopefully conflict does occur and can be learned from. Affirmation and resolution also occur and tell the ACoA that there is hope that they may be able to do this outside the treatment setting.

Experiential methods — This refers to methods such as role play, re-enactment of scenes from past or present family situations, using stand-ins rather than actual family members. The use of psychodrama, Gestalt, sculpture and other experiential techniques (in contrast with more traditional talk therapy), has several advantages in the inpatient setting. These methods tend to bypass the ACoA distrust of words and tap into the feeling life of the person. More work can be done in less time as emotional discharge is stimulated. Rather than talking about how one felt during a major loss, group members actually feel and discharge the grief. Such methods do not eliminate the need for talk or processing, but emphasis is on the emotional experience, rather than the thought process. Later in outpatient counseling, it is necessary to talk about options, changes, etc.

Limitations of Inpatient Treatment

There are several limitations to inpatient treatment which should be mentioned. It is impossible to know all there is to know about a person when contact is brief. No matter how thorough an intake interview, or how much information is exchanged between therapists, important things can be missed. A therapist can only know what you tell them and what you show them. If they have good instincts, and a solid knowledge of this disease, they can assume a lot about you in a short time, but they will still be limited.

Those who have been treated in a highly intense, emotionally charged inpatient setting may have difficulty returning to a traditional therapy group unless they are adequately prepared.

Joe, who was unable to find a therapist trained in experiential methods, made this comment one year after his inpatient treatment.

"Even though I really trusted my outpatient ACoA group, I was sometimes frustrated with the lack of intensity. It took me a few months to accept the fact that maybe I didn't need it after all and was just looking for the Quick Fix."

Aftercare is more than essential; it is the key to the success of any inpatient program, and must be emphasized from beginning to end. Without adequate follow-up, the individual will be left feeling abandoned and unable to function in the real world. Fortunately, follow-up study has shown that a very small number, 10%, of those treated, do not follow through with professional help after inpatient ACoA treatment. Of the 10%, however, most report being active in 12-step meetings without any professional counseling.

Cost is another limitation since most short-term inpatient programs are not as yet reimbursable by insurance. This does not seem to be a major deterrent to Adult Children who are determined to find quality help regardless of expense or inconvenience. Progress is being made in recognition of co-dependency as a legitimate diagnosable illness, which is gradually improving the situation.

Outpatient Treatment

Outpatient Co-dependency treatment generally offers both individual and group counseling, frequently including couples and family therapy as well. At this time public agencies are beginning to develop services for Adult Children, having focused for years on treating only addiction. Private practitioners and treatment centers are another good resource. Generally good quality therapists and programs will have established a reputation within the 12-step groups and you will be able to find out what is available by asking individuals after a meeting. If the same names keep coming up, they are probably quite good.

If you have no idea how to find a therapist, it helps to view yourself as a consumer purchasing a service. You have the right to ask questions, but try to be diplomatic and not put the therapist in a position of defending his or her skills. My own bias is that most often a woman benefits more from a female therapist, a man with a male. This is not always the case, but it is something to consider, and it may make a difference in the long run.

Degrees are not as important as training and experience with your type of problem. A directive therapist, who is willing to give you assignments, directs honest feedback and at times alternatives, is preferable over a more passive, "laid-back" type. Adult Children and Grandchildren are not full of ideas when it comes to alternatives and decision-making. You need all the help you can get until you are able to go it alone. Someone who is willing to talk about themselves a little may help you to feel more comfortable, although too much self-disclosure is not good either. You want to get your money's worth.

Ask questions like "How do you work with clients? How long does it normally take? What do you expect of me? How much will this cost?"

You have a right to know these things and will have a better chance of sticking with it if you know what to expect in advance.

Outpatient programs may begin with an educational program or incorporate this through reading assignments, films, etc. If this is not part of the program, you may want to do this on your own. Experience has shown that although individual therapy for a period of time prepares the ACoA for treatment, group works best for most.

The exception is someone who is having difficulty with paranoia or consistent misinterpretation of what is said to and around them. This person may need to spend more time in individual therapy before beginning group. Victims of severe abuse may need to continue individual therapy along with group or for a period of time after completion of group therapy to fully recover from the possible flashbacks and residual feelings that may occur.

Emotional discharge can be accomplished in outpatient therapy as long as there are the conditions of safety and protection referred to previously. This can be very helpful in speeding up the process. Without any discharge throughout the course of treatment it will be very difficult to change lifetime patterns. Feelings tend to overpower insight and despite knowledge of what needs to change, we tend to be strongly motivated and driven by our feelings which have been repressed.

Several years ago when I was doing outpatient therapy with co-dependents in a small community program, I met Betsy who was the wife of an alcoholic. She was caught in the cycle of threatening to leave her abusive alcoholic husband, occasionally doing so but always returning.

She had what I called the "I knows". "I know I should follow through. I know it's hurting my children. I know I need to take care of myself . . . But . . ." Betsy had been attending Al-Anon for four years, sponsoring others and helping to set up new groups in the community. She was painfully aware that her life was exactly like her mother's had been. She was an Adult Child, absolutely incapable of change using insight alone. Knowing what was wrong did not help until Betsy began to address and express the emotional pain — anger toward her father for his abuse and her mother for her passivity, fear that she or her children would be harmed, grief at the loss of the dream family she had hoped for. Group therapy allowed Betsy to begin this process, and eventually to make substantial changes.

Any therapy for Adult Children and Grandchildren must involve ongoing education about relating to others in daily life. This is where outpatient has a distinct advantage in that opportunities based on problems in daily living can come up and teaching can occur spontaneously, even during group therapy. For example: How to express anger, assertiveness-training, parenting, intimacy, sex, handling money, dating, job problems, handling criticism, etc. This education may take place as formal workshops for one or more groups or a small part of a group session spent discussing new ways of acting.

Outpatient therapy can provide almost instant feedback to the client on day-to-day events. Patterns of behavior can be observed and eventually changed with feedback and direction. With the emphasis on peer support through 12-step meetings, a dependency will not be likely. Clients need to know that therapy is time-limited and the goal is to learn how to do these things without needing to pay for professional services. Practice within a healthy support system outside of group will assure this.

It is sometimes necessary to leave a group session while you are still hurting, feeling sad, hurt, etc. If you have a support system, this can be a means of coping with bad feelings in between groups. If you leave group feeling great every week, it probably means you aren't doing much changing!

Because one of the few limitations of outpatient therapy is the difficulty in bringing about emotional discharge in a safe environment with limited time each week, the ideal treatment plan would be a combination of both inpatient and outpatient treatment. The timing of each is individual, decided with the help of a therapist. It may also be necessary to take part in couples counseling once you have done some work on your identity and ability to communicate needs. Couples work is less effective if you are not yet able to state who you are and what you want in your life. Family therapy can be helpful in rebuilding the family system, changing present family rules and patterns and developing parenting skills.

Treatment Issues

There are some things an ACoA/GCoA can expect to focus on in any treatment setting. Although the timing and approach may be somewhat individual, most co-dependents will at one time or another face these issues.

Identifying and Learning to Express Feelings

The fact that this is a problem does not need to be restated. Betsy, for example, was a "crier" but could not identify the feeling behind the tears. She was never able to acknowledge anger. In group she was asked continually how she was feeling and was often told by group members when she looked or sounded angry. Eventually she was able to observe these things in herself and learn through role-playing how to express anger.

The process of change is a gradual one, and therapy, along with exposure to others who deal with feelings openly, can help. Modeling on the part of the therapist and other group members demonstrates the skill of expressing feelings and gives permission to take risks.

When feelings begin to emerge, particularly about the past, they may come in a flood, uninvited. This is what makes the initial stages of treatment difficult, in that it may interfere with normal functioning. Defenses like isolation, humor, overwork, etc., do not work to cover up the depths of pain that surface. Most often we continue to function at an acceptable level, and get through this temporary crisis.

Eventually a greater degree of control is present and the ACoA finds that he/she can choose to express feelings when and where he wants. It becomes posssible to postpone the tears until it is safer and appropriate without fear of having to "stuff" them once again. It becomes possible to feel joy and experience intimate connections with loved ones.

Changing belief systems can over time change feelings. Although it may not have been possible to change the fact that Betsy was angry, she was able during her time in group to change some of her beliefs, expectations and attitudes and prevent the same things from bothering her over and over. This intellectual restructuring is a part of the process.

Identifying Abuse, Expressing the Pain and Understanding

This process, detailed in the previous chapter, is a thread woven through the treatment experience. It begins in therapy but continues long after. There is no event. The process includes identifying and discharging the pain, restructuring our thinking and behavior and gradually letting go and forgiving.

Intimacy Issues

Surveying ACoAs one year after treatment indicates that intimacy is still the Number 1 concern and difficulty.

It is definitely an ongoing process. In treatment a great deal of re-educating takes place about what intimacy is and how to accomplish it.

Many ACoA/GCoAs, having intimacy confused with sex or enmeshed relationships, need to begin by learning how to be a friend.

Jeff, the "average ACoA" mentioned earlier, was unaware of the need to establish emotional closeness in an intimate relationship. He had never developed a friendship with a woman and was hoping that sex would bring about the emotional bond he was seeking.

A treatment group can provide a safe environment to learn new things since romantic involvements are prohibited between group members. With this assurance, the individual may get close through emotional honesty without the negative consequences. They learn how much to trust from sharing and seeing the results. Friendshps outside of the treatment group may begin in 12-step meetings with the same sex, and then gradually include a circle of friends of both sexes. This process is exactly what "normal" people go through in adolescence.

Intimacy occurs everyday of our lives in recovery with our children, friends, family and intimate partner. It often begins in recovery with honest, open communication on a feeling level and develops into appropriate affection and emotional investment as the particular relationship indicates.

Without this learning process there will be no comfortable, healthy sexual relationship. Once fear of intimacy is addressed and, to a degree, conquered, sexual intimacy will happen naturally. That is not to say there is no work involved. Many ACoAs/GCoAs have a history of pain to overcome, some of it over sexual abuse, which will occasionally get in the way. With honest communication and a willingness to seek ongoing help as needed, most of the blocks to intimacy can be overcome.

Other Addictions and Compulsions

It is difficult to find an Adult Child or Grandchild of an Alcoholic without one or more addictions. Even those who are in recovery from chemical dependency struggle with other addictions as well. They may include food, sex, work, gambling, relationships, spending, smoking, sports and numerous others. The question for professionals and the ACoA/GCoA is whether treatment for co-dependency is enough to handle the "other addictions".

The answer is yes for many and no for a few. Depending on how far the addiction has progressed, additional treatment, specific to the problem, may be necessary.

Persons with eating disorders, such as bulimia and anorexia, would need to address these areas specifically and such treatment would include medical evaluation. Later stages of sexual addiction generally require special treatment as well. Inpatient treatment would be the preferred method in these cases, but good individual and group therapy where the specific addiction is discussed with knowledgeable professionals might also be effective.

In most cases treating the co-dependency, releasing old rage and grief, learning to express feelings and utilizing a support system will adequately address the other addictions. Twelve-step support, e.g., Overeaters Anonymous, Gamblers Anonymous, etc., will give individuals an opportunity for direction and support in maintaining abstinence.

Abstinence is a term used most often in reference to life without drugs or alcohol. It can also be used to describe the first step in dealing with any addiction. ACoA/GCoAs can make a commitment to abstain from any person, activity, behavior, substance or place, which results in a compulsive cycle over which they feel no choice.

An example might be someone with a spending addiction who decides to abstain from shopping in any large shopping center or mall but feels capable of doing so in a supermarket. The commitment and a personal definition of abstinence can be decided with the help of a therapist and the support of a therapy group and possibly an appropriate 12-step group, e.g., Debtors Anonymous.

The period of time when the addictive behavior is not available as an option for dealing with feelings will be one of unbelievable growth. Once the person is forced by choice to face feelings, rather than repress them in familiar ways, they will begin to make significant internal and external changes.

Trust Issues

Although the ACoA/GCoA is reluctant to trust based on past experiences of hurt, abandonment or disappointment, there will come a time in treatment when a conscious decision to trust must be made. This may happen several times at deeper and deeper levels. It is the responsibility of the therapist and facility to guarantee safety, confidentiality and protection from harm. Once this is in place, the decision to trust or not to trust is in the hands of the client.

Granted, it may take time to get to the point of trust, but it isn't just going to happen one day because those around you earned it. There will never be a point in time when there is no risk of hurt, pain or human error. In order to benefit from treatment, the ACoA/GCoA needs to trust anyway.

Spirituality

Most recovering alcoholics and co-dependents would attest to the need for spiritual healing in order to have a satisfying recovery and life. For many this does not involve organized religion. It does involve development of a sense of a Higher Power, some higher purpose to life beyond our own wishes and desires.

Gradually, each individual through their own spiritual search, trial and error, meditation and prayer, may find and define their own personal Higher Power. This process brings about a stronger sense of values and beliefs about the purpose of life and provides a support system of a spiritual nature. This support is with the individual in the quiet moments of the day when no external support is available or needed.

With it comes the return of the Spirit of oneself, the spirit which was present at birth but was gradually extinguished throughout a painful life. The will to live, not only physically, but emotionally and mentally, can be restored as a result of the spiritual journey.

It seems that very few professionals are equipped or comfortable with this essential part of the treatment process. Spirituality is not something magical that comes after treatment. It, too, involves hard work, study, experimentation with new ways of thinking, attempts at prayer when full of doubt, meditation times spent pondering one's personal definition of Higher Power.

Many ACoA/GCoAs have had extremely negative religious experiences, which become obstacles to recovery unless they are addressed in treatment. Introducing, and perhaps modeling the concept of Higher Power, in the therapy setting can guide a client into this emotionally charged area. Decisions to utilize formal religion are best left to the individual and need not be part of the treatment process.

The very best therapists I have known are those who are aware of the spiritual guidance from which they draw to do their work. They wear their spirituality rather than preach it. It is something one can observe and sense. A skilled therapist is aware that most ACoA/GCoAs are not ready to address spirituality early in treatment. But hopefully when they start searching for it, it will be part of the treatment experience.

Play and Balance

People who spend their free time writing books are generally not the best authorities on the subject of play. Many ACoA/GCoAs are very willing to work hard at anything including their treatment, but need to be coerced into playing. Therapists may give crazy assignments like, "Go fly a kite, or roller-skate before next week's group."

A few words about play from one who has a dreaded fear of losing control or looking stupid: There are many forms of play. Some of us get extreme pleasure from just being around playful people on a regular basis. Some people love playing crazy games. Some love to sing, dance and read poetry. Whatever it is that fits for you, the point is that life is meant to be enjoyed.

ACoA/GCoAs often live their lives getting ready for the time when the pleasure will come. The old tape of "work first, play later" runs in our heads. Treatment groups can teach each other to laugh and to discover what is fun in each person. Non-competitive games, which do not humiliate, shame or violate boundaries, can teach the co-dependent to enjoy being with people, laughing, touching and playing without fear of ridicule or harm. This is an important part of treatment.

Extreme thinkers have difficulty balancing play and work (including treatment work), and may fluctuate from one to the other exclusively before arriving at a comfortable compromise. Once again a therapy group, along with a 12-step support network, can model and support change, encouraging a balanced recovery.

Self-esteem

Treatment is an essential part of improving one's concept of themselves. It is a huge undertaking, taking many years to accomplish. The more damaged the individual has been, the more difficult the task. The important thing is that it can be done.

The treatment setting can serve as a learning lab for co-dependents to discover what they really look like to the rest of the world. Believing there is anything good to see is half the battle. The ACoA/GCoA needs honest feedback, not only strokes, along with the consistent affirmation that "Whatever you are is okay."

The safety of a therapy group allows the individual to let in some of the good things without the fear of being rejected later. Although the feedback of the therapist is important, it is not as valuable as that of one's peers. They represent the rest of the world where eventually the person must return. Knowing my therapist loves me is not as reassuring as knowing that this group, who has seen me at my worst, loves me *unconditionally.*

The long-term progress takes place during and after treatment in the restructuring of environment and relationships in which the co-dependent lives. We must surround ourselves with people who value and affirm. We cannot improve self-concept while surrounded with negativity and abuse.

The Role of Self-help

I have consciously avoided identifying one 12-step group as the most effective for Adult Children and/or Grandchildren. My follow-up with treated Adult Children from different parts of the country indicates that each has found their own "best" way, whether AA, Al-Anon, ACoA, or a combination of all. The choice depends not only on the individual, but also on the community. Development of quality Al-Anon is still not guaranteed in every area of the country. ACoA meetings are even less developed. Some areas have had successful, positive, healthy groups functioning for several years, others are still focused on the "problems" and have few members with the "solutions".

Despite the struggle for identity of Adult Children's groups, my personal bias is that a group founded on the steps and traditions of Al-Anon and AA has a better chance of providing the answers and direction for a new way of life.

There is no better means to discovery of a Higher Power than within a 12-step program. Some will find the Al-Anon groups in their area more helpful than ACoA. Recovering alcoholics report that they are more able to use AA effectively if they have also addressed their ACoA issues.

Grandchildren present a unique problem in this regard. Although they qualify for Al-Anon in that they have a "problem of alcoholism in a relative or friend", they may struggle with belonging. It is possible to find a meeting or meetings which focus more on present issues, relationships, letting go, detachment, etc., without talking specifically about any alcoholic in the family. Therapy can serve the need for disclosure and introspection about the past. It is also possible to find a sponsor who understands your situation and will not judge you as "too healthy" to be there.

As Grandchildren of Alcoholics share at meetings they may discover others who may have found the program through marriage to an alcoholic, or an addicted child, but are also Grandchildren trying to put the pieces together. As we begin to disclose openly, it will be more common and less uncomfortable to be a Grandchild among ACoAs.

When we focus on present issues, there is no way to distinguish an ACoA from a Grandchild. Look for the similarities and remember you are entitled to be there.

It is my belief that self-help alone is not enough for the ACoA/GCoA in most cases. The process of dramatic change might be accomplished with rigorous application of the 12-steps, but the program has certain limitations which slow down the process, leaving the individual in pain possibly years longer than necessary. AA, Al-Anon, and ACoA were not designed to confront, give direct feedback, promote and support emotional discharge, teach specific living skills like assertiveness, etc. Persons trying to grow in the program without the aid of therapy will often try to get these things from meetings, only to feel discounted and frustrated. It is not realistic to expect other ACoAs to provide that kind of specialized help. It is not necessary to suffer and struggle for years when help is available.

SUMMARY

Adult Children, Grandchildren and those from other types of dysfunctional homes can all be treated effectively in the same settings. It is important for the ACoA/GCoA to make the connection to alcoholism in the family.

Services for this group are developing and expanding rapidly all over the country, making it essential that the individual know what he/she is looking for and whether or not it is quality. A combination of education, support, inpatient co-dependency treatment and outpatient therapy is recommended.

Among the issues faced in treatment are identifying and expressing feelings, intimacy, other addictions and compulsions, trust, spirituality, play and balance, and self-esteem. Although these require long-term effort, treatment will give specific guidance and direction to aid progress.

Self-help in the form of 12-step groups is a vital ingredient to the treatment process. It can be the insurance policy that makes treatment "stick". The development of an ongoing support system is a means of maintaining and continuing growth beyond treatment. Self-help, however, is not intended to be treatment or therapy.

_____ Chapter 6 _____

The Recovery Process

Personal recovery for a Grandchild of an Alcoholic, Adult Child, spouse or anyone surviving a dsyfunctional home begins with treatment but extends into a lifetime process of growth and change. The goal is not to come up with a perfect formula for what makes a healthy person and then mass produce health. It is really a personal journey of discovery of who it is we were meant and created to be in the first place. It is fairly easy to recognize when we're on the right track because it will feel unusually comfortable, despite the occasional pain that may accompany the changes.

My observations and personal experiences have contributed to the compiling of a list of road signs or guideposts which seem to be present in the process of growth for many of us. The order in which they occur, along with the time frame involved, is very individual. Many start the journey and take breaks and side trips along the way. Some cling desperately to one path and hastily move through each obstacle unaverted. Others attempt many paths, going back to more familiar ones periodically for comfort and security of having been there before.

The most fascinating part of the journey is that no one knows the destination! The more determined we are to arrive at a specific place, the less likely we are to get there. One key element is our willingness to be open to the possibilities, the doors and windows which appear along the way. The journey really has nothing to do with illness at all. It is the challenge of becoming a whole person, the task that is before every human being.

In describing stages of recovery, I will be using the example of a recovering Grandchild named Doris since her experience seems to be fairly typical.

Doris discovered her co-dependency after she had divorced her alcoholic husband and was referred to Al-Anon by a family service counselor. While in Al-Anon, she began to see that she was not the first co-dependent woman in her family. Her grandmothers on both sides had lived through similar situations. Although she could not call herself an ACoA, Doris was sure there was little difference between herself and those who had an alcoholic parent.

Doris sought treatment with a private therapist who had a group for Adult Children and over a period of one year began to make gradual changes.

Recovery Stages

I have divided the process of change into three stages, each with their own tasks and challenges.

STAGE I — What's Wrong With Me?

This stage may actually be going on for a lifetime for some who have always felt different from the rest of the world. Doris was conscious most of her life of a feeling of being "less than" others. Although her family looked "normal", she often experienced the sense that there was something missing. She felt guilty that she did not really believe that her parents loved her, despite the outward gestures that were made.

When Doris began to attend Al-Anon, at first only because of her alcoholic marriage, she immediately felt right at home. It took some time before she began to put the pieces together from her family history. Fortunately, Doris was aware of the alcoholism in her family, even though she herself did not live with it. She felt a great deal of relief almost immediately when she was able to see that she did not create this problem all by herself. She now knew that the problem was alcoholism and co-dependency and not her poor choice of a spouse.

Finding out what is really wrong can relieve a great deal of the guilt and shame that accompanies this disease. With that relief comes the energy to move on to begin the process of change.

The tasks of this stage include:

1. Identification of the Problem

For most Adult Children the moment of truth is occurring as part of an educational process. The new awareness of the damage done to children of alcoholics has reached out through the media, professional conferences, books and to a great extent word of mouth.

The awareness of being an Adult Child often comes without any conscious effort when it is least expected. Some individuals may even have done everything they could to *avoid* finding out when suddenly the light comes on.

I have witnessed this event with professionals who are attending conferences or seminars to improve their skills in working with "those other people"; recovering alcoholics who are confronted by a friend in AA about their ACoA issues; men and women whose siblings have been treated, all suddenly realizing they too have the problem.

This realization can be as startling as a lightning bolt or so subtle that it takes years to sink in. Once it hits, however, it is very hard to turn back, pretending you don't know. With identification comes a sense of belonging, being understood, part of a larger group who knows what your life has been like. This may be the first time in a lifetime of isolation when this belonging is felt.

A sense of relief is experienced knowing that "I didn't bring this on myself — it is not only my problem!" A search for more information begins, with the hope that with knowledge will come more relief.

When the "light bulb" came on for Doris, she felt a compelling urge to share her insight with others. She armed herself with the most current reading material on the family disease of alcoholism and began to approach her family and her ex-husband with the good news that they too had been affected and could benefit from treatment and Al-Anon. Needless to say, they did not view this as good news and Doris was "sidetracked" in her own recovery for a few months, trying to cope with the resulting rejection and frustration.

Once you have discovered what the real problem is, it is very hard to turn back to resuming the denial and old ways of thinking. Even when Doris was "slipping" into fixing her family, she was assured by watching others in the program and her therapy group that she could change herself, and there was hope for her future, if not for her family of origin.

For Grandchildren of Alcoholics identification has not been very easy. Authorities in the addiction field are just beginning to include the multigenerational view in their training and educating. Most Grandchildren, like Doris, fall into treatment accidentally and discover their families' co-dependency and alcoholism in the process.

The good news is that each recovering Grandchild will undoubtedly share their discoveries with others and hopefully more and more Grandchildren will identify their co-dependency.

2. Breaking the "No Talk Rule"

It is not enough to know what the problem is if it is never shared with others. Many ACoA/GCoAs have grown up knowing what was wrong, keeping the painful secret to themselves in the belief that talking would not make it any different. They were told to leave the past behind them, only to discover in their adult lives that it came along anyway.

Learning how to say out loud "I am an ACoA/GCoA" is not as important as learning to let others see the inside you. Sharing your bad days and your good days with those who care about you is where it begins. Telling the whole story, instead of what you have edited into an acceptable form, leaves you open to the feedback, support and suggestions of others.

Years of keeping secrets led the co-dependent to censor his/her own thoughts, presenting only what looks okay or will be least upsetting to others. In the process they eliminate opportunities to get close to others, letting them in emotionally and becoming intimate. Some ACoA/GCoAs do an awful lot of talking but rarely share any part of themselves. Their comments are limited to information about other people, events, facts and opinions.

For Doris breaking the "no talk rule" meant telling it all to a few important people in her life. She began to take calculated risks to share herself with others, discovering through this practice that she not only survived but that she felt better about herself.

At first she was careful about who she shared openly with, using her therapist and her group exclusively.

Gradually she began to talk more at meetings about the daily things that upset her. The hardest part was to begin to share herself with friends and to actually let them know the real person. This change was quickly noticed by those close to her, and Doris found that people actually appreciated it when she wasn't so well put together. They felt more comfortable being human when she did the same.

When beginning to open up, it is not a good idea to take a leap of faith and tell everyone everything! Some people can be trusted, some cannot. It may be wise to check it out first with something not as important — for instance, tell a friend you are going to counseling. Wait for the reaction before you move on to bigger things.

Discretion, especially in small communities, is just plain sensible. It is not sick or dysfunctional to want to protect your parents or grandparents from the possible trauma of public knowledge of the alcoholism in the family. You will find many safe places to discuss these sensitive issues once you have become more comfortable.

3. Asking for help

This is not a task that is done once and then finished with. Admitting "powerlessness" is the first step in Alcoholics Anonymous and other 12-step programs because it is necessary to see that you cannot do it all alone before change can begin. It is not necessary to ignore personal intelligence, experience and strength, but an honest look at your life so far will tell you those things are not enough. Your way is not working!

Professional help may be one of your choices at this point, but that isn't the only task in this step. For Doris, who had survived by "doing it alone" for her entire life, it was easier to depend on a professional than on friends and family. She was encouraged to reach out to others on a daily basis and began with simple things like asking for a ride to a meeting, a cup of coffee, calling a friend when she needed to talk.

Where asking for help was not even an option for Doris previously, she began to see it as a way of life, rather than something she only did on the bad days when she was desperate. She found that some of her friends were accustomed to "being helped", rather than helping and they drifted away somewhat. The friendships which were based on mutual support grew.

After a few months of working on this area, Doris had three very special friends who were very important to her on the good *and* bad days. She previously had had a dozen friends who did not know her and were not able to help when she did reach out.

This step is an acknowledgement that you have needs, too. You probably don't know yet what they are, but with practice, they will become clearer. In therapy you learn to reach out before making decisions impulsively. You may bring a problem to group for their input, instead of suffering it out alone. You may eventually admit to your spouse and children that you are human and your needs count, but this will take a little time. Change often begins outside of the family situation where practice is safer and less risky.

The "compulsive caretakers"who have surrounded themselves with needy dependent people will have some housecleaning to do. Renegotiating some day-to-day responsibilities and learning to say "No" more often enables you to take the time you need for yourself. Saying things like "I don't know" or "I won't be available" gives the message that you don't have all the answers for others.

STAGE II — Who Am I?

Self-discovery is a long-term process for anyone, but those from healthy homes have a head start on the Adult

Child or Grandchild of Alcoholics. Having developed a pseudo-self (or false self) it is necessary to build a new identity made up of personal needs, preferences, feelings and choices based on genuine soul-searching and much experimentation.

The tasks of this stage include:

1. Learning Self-caring as a Way of Life

Even without knowing clearly what you like, want or need, the challenge of trying new things and experimenting with what feels good to you can be an enjoyable one.

After a few months in therapy, following the example and encouragement of others in her group and in Al-Anon, Doris began to pay closer attention to her own needs. At first the physical was the most obvious — starting to eat right, wearing attractive clothes, trying some makeup. She also noticed the stressful pace she had been keeping and tried to slow down, allowing some time for "smelling the roses". She discovered that she really enjoyed the drive to work when she wasn't in a hurry and also that her attitude was better when she got there. Doris even decided to wear her seat-belt in the car as a symbol of her love for herself.

Although she had always been conscientious about her children's dental and medical needs, she had not had a check-up in years — not wanting to spend the money on herself. These things, too, began to change.

Tuning in to her emotional needs was not as easy, but with the feedback of friends and those in the program, she became more aware of when she needed things like being alone, a good cry, a friend to talk to, some fun and laughter. The key was to learn to listen to the little voice inside, instead of staying so busy that she never noticed what her inner self needed.

Since therapy was bringing up some very painful issues and feelings from her past, it was important for Doris to balance these out with joy. She learned to have fun with her own children in simple daily activities. She resumed some interesting hobbies she had given up during her husband's active drinking and made a point of talking to a friend at least once a day.

There is a vast difference between being selfish in the negative sense and being self-caring. The practice of taking care of oneself gives your family and friends the message that you are a responsible healthy person who does not have to manipulate or play games to get his/her needs met. It is the best way to teach others that you deserve to be treated respectfully; after all, that's how you treat yourself. It does not mean that you stop caring for others, only that you are putting yourself first some of the time.

Every parent is aware of the many times we must put our children's needs ahead of our own. This also happens in marriages and any significant friendship. The important change that happens in recovery is that we can choose to put our needs aside temporarily because someone is important to us. We are no longer acting out of guilt or obligation. It actually feels good to put others first, as long as you are also meeting your own needs most of the time.

Once you begin to discover some of your needs, learning to communicate them without becoming aggressive is important. Deciding on your personal limits is also a means of self-caring. Instead of waiting for others to see that you have "had it", recognize your own internal signals of fatigue and frustration and express yourself.

It may take a little time for friends and family to become accustomed to you taking care of yourself. When you notice that they seem confused and sometimes annoyed with your behavior, it is a sure sign you are changing. Co-dependents tend to rush to extremes in making changes and may suddenly appear very self-centered and then totally selfless. Balance comes with practice.

2. Feeling the Pain and Sharing It As It Occurs

Our feelings make up to a great extent who we are. Simply changing behavior will not work if we attempt to deny our feelings. In coping with feelings two things are happening simultaneously — old feelings of pain bubble up to the surface as you become ready to face them and present-day feelings become apparent in normal responses to daily events. Both may be relatively new experiences for the ACoA/GCoA in recovery.

When an individual has survived a painful past, it does not suddenly come into memory in therapy to be addressed in its entirety. The memories return slowly, over months and even years, sometimes in what feels like floods, but never all at once.

It has been said that "God doesn't give us anything we're not ready to handle." It helps to view the pain as something useful, a way out of the past. Remembering painful things and openly acknowledging the anger, fear and grief seems to speed up the process and open new doors for change.

Doris had been married to an alcoholic for 15 years. Their relationship was abusive from the very beginning, with a great deal of fighting, both verbal and physical. Doris was raised with an absence of affection and intimacy in her family of origin. In therapy the theme of emotional abandonment was a recurring one for Doris. As other group members would share their histories in therapy, or when a newcomer would come in to Al-Anon, Doris found herself reliving some of her own pain.

When one of her Al-Anon friends, whose husband was in recovery, had a baby, Doris remembered vividly the birth of her son, a very painful and lonely time for her with a drunk absent husband unable to share the important event with her. With this memory she was able to cry openly, sharing her grief with several friends over the course of two or three days. The grief was not paralyzing. She continued to function and was even helpful to her friend when she arrived home with her new baby. Doris was told by those who cared, and she could also feel within herself, that healing was taking place. Over the course of her treatment and even years later, Doris had many other experiences like this one and was no longer devastated by them.

When memories return, they become less intense with each recurrence. Memories are often brought on by special dates, anniversaries or holidays. Depending upon the severity of the situation recalled, it can feel just like the day it happened years before. The pain will not last as long but you will need a great deal of support in the beginning of this healing period. The reason it is necessary to re-experience these feelings is that you were not permitted to express the pain when the event took place and have, in a sense, stored the feelings until now.

When pain surfaces, it may be tempting to use some familiar addictive or compulsive behavior to cope with it. Abstaining from the things you use to cover feelings will aid in moving you through, rather than around, the pain. It will not go away if you continue to repress it with food, sex, relationships, work, nicotine, etc.

As the intensity decreases you may learn to postpone expressing the pain until you are in a more appropriate setting. Crying at work is very uncomfortable and embarrassing. This postponement is not repression. It is healthy and can prevent further damage to your self-esteem and your relationships with co-workers, children, etc. Some places are better than others for expressing feelings. Once the major discharge has taken place in treatment, later you will feel much more in control of when and where you let go emotionally.

3. Feel the Fear and Guilt and Do It Anyway

As we attempt to change behaviors which have been comfortably established in our lives, it is natural for feelings of fear and sometimes guilt to surface. This does not have to be a major obstacle to change and can be worked through by expressing it openly and moving forward anyway.

Many co-dependents have developed a long list of things they "can't" do by the time they reach treatment. This may include driving alone, being in high places, speaking in a group, talking about themselves, crying real tears, being assertive with the boss, eating spinach, etc. It was necessary while growing up in a painful environment to be very protective of oneself, careful not to risk losing what little security and self-esteem might be present.

When a new identity is forming, it is almost necessary to erase this list and begin slowly one step at a time to take each one on as a challenge. This may take years, and personally I have chosen to keep a few of my fears — like roller coasters. The important thing is to reduce the number of "I can'ts" so that we may live richer, freer, more fulfilling lives.

Many of these new things will not affect anyone around you, except in a positive way. You will be a lot more interesting and fun to be with. Some of our changes, however, bring negative responses from those closest to us and require great effort to get past.

Doris had been conditioned by her co-dependent mother to put the needs and wishes of others ahead of her own. Whenever she did something nice for herself, especially if it inconvenienced or upset someone else, she felt a black cloud of guilt come over her. Sometimes she could even hear her mother's voice saying, "You are being selfish! What kind of a mother are you?!" Her children, two boys aged 10 and 12, were aware of her "guilt button" and pressed it at every opportunity.

As Doris began to set limits and stick to them, at the same time taking more time to take care of herself, her sons reacted loudly. They began trying things like saying they wanted to live with their father (who was still drinking), or that they didn't like her anymore since she had become mean and self-centered.

Once again, Doris had been prepared, at least partially, by those who had blazed this trail ahead of her in Al-Anon. When she shared her guilt and fear of abandonment with others at meetings, they assured her it would pass. This was just her children's natural resistance to change. With the group's frequent support and encouragement, she was able to stick to her new, healthier parenting, and the boys began to prefer this method to the old inconsistency they were used to.

Fear and guilt can be healthy feelings if we use them as an opportunity to stop and think once more before we act. They are telling us to be careful, check out how important this is, consider its impact on others, move slowly until we are more comfortable. Those are good things to look at.

Some co-dependents read these feelings as *stop, don't do it!*, and never move another inch further. Looking at fear and guilt as caution lights, rather than red lights, will keep you moving forward.

What do you do with the feelings while you're changing? Talk about them, share with others that you aren't sure of yourself, ask people to be with you while you do new things. Use your therapy group to rehearse new ways of communicating with loved ones, employers, children. Practice will take away the terror of something new, and taking action will eventually relieve the guilt. Don't expect guilt to disappear quickly just because you are sure you're doing the right thing. It has become such an automatic response, it will take time to finally go away.

STAGE III — Who Do I Want to BE?

At this stage major changes are possible and have already begun, probably without the use of formal therapy. The label of co-dependent or ACoA/GCoA is less important. You have begun the larger process of living and loving.

Tasks in this stage include:

1. Viewing Recovery as an Adventure Rather than a Goal

In the earlier stages there may have been a tendency to keep a long negative inventory of "things to be worked on". The belief may have been that once you eliminated most of these character defects, you would be okay and healthy. In this stage it has occurred to you that the list is now made up of both positive and negative things, but it isn't getting any shorter. The process of change and growth is an ongoing one.

When a new character defect is discovered, it is seen as an opportunity to learn more about yourself, eliminate some troublesome habit, get feedback and strengthen your identity. With stronger self-esteem you no longer believe there should be no defects. Your goal is not to eliminate them but to become aware and make choices about them. You are no longer changing because you are unacceptable to yourself or others, but because you really enjoy growing.

Once Doris had completed her treatment, she continued to use meetings as an important support. She had other friends through work and church, but felt the need for frequent reminders of the steps and really enjoyed the social aspect of meetings as well. She had developed a strong "family of choice". Her relationships with her own family were still a bit strained and superficial, but not a major source of pain for Doris.

She was now confronted with putting it all into practice but felt quite confident that although she would not ever be perfect, she was a pretty special person. She became more aware of the fact that she was not very different from the rest of the "normies" and that she had a lot of very special people in her life. As problems occurred, parenting teen-age boys, beginning to date, making difficult career decisions, Doris did not view them as setbacks, but as life. She put her energy into the loving relationships she had, and into improving herself with each opportunity for growth.

Knowing herself put Doris in a position of strength in her relationships. She was no longer at the mercy of people who wanted to manipulate or abuse. She was able to present herself honestly, willing to assume responsibility for her own actions and feelings. She had moved beyond *recovering* and into *living*.

2. Self-forgiveness

Many ACoA/GCoAs have tried to forgive others without stopping first to forgive themselves. Sometimes it is easier to see and accept a reasonable explanation for the crazy behavior of others but not our own. Forgiveness is a gradual change in attitude and feelings, not a moment of truth or a sudden realization. It is truly a spiritual process of getting centered with oneself. It involves standing back with some objectivity and looking at the choices you have made, realizing that you did the best you could do at the time with the tools available to you.

Doris had a great deal of pain about raising her children with a drunk father. She regretted her choice of a husband, and then felt badly that she had stayed in it for so long, further damaging her children. When she took an honest look at her preparation for marriage, the model she was raised with in her own family, she could see clearly that she had no other choice but to follow the family pattern. Without all of the work she had done on herself up to this point, she could not have forgiven herself. However, knowing it intellectually, and believing it in her heart, were two different things.

With this soul search comes a sense of peace, a comfort with the past, a belief that it was as it was meant to be. You come to believe that you are a better person for the experiences you have had. For many it has meant facing a real choice between life and death. In choosing life, there is a strong desire to make it the best life possible. This desire would not have been there if not for the struggle.

You may now view yourself as partially responsible, especially for choices made as an adult. You do not need to blame and beat yourself for those choices. You have learned new ways to avoid the people and situations which hurt you before. You put yourself in affirming places, with people who like and respect you, where smiles and laughter, touch and tears are equally safe.

The voice of the child within, the playful spontaneous spirit of you, can be heard. This does not require regression to a childish state, just a willingness to be still and listen to the voice that says "Go for it!"

You have learned to use a support system of persons who will affirm you when you are being unkind to yourself. When you revert to the familiar behavior of self-blaming, your support system will remind you of how special you are and how far you have come. It will be a place to "check it out", rather than relying only on your own voice. Self-forgiveness is not a constant, it requires reinforcement from outside us and will not hold up well when exposed to negativity and illness. We need to take very good care of ourselves. A support system will make it easier to do this.

The approval-seeking, which used to be a way of life, is now in a different form. We still care what others think, especially if we respect and value the relationship. But we care equally about our own evaluation of our behavior. A shift occurs where we begin to first ask ourselves "How did I do? Am I okay?" We can trust that the answer will be honest and fair.

If this isn't enough, we turn to those who love us and ask again. The difference is that we do not draw our self-esteem from others, but rather from inside ourselves. The validation we need the most is from that little voice that is with us all the time. The mental committee of negative voices, who used to criticize and debate every action and choice, are almost silent.

3. *Other Forgiveness*

This is not a day or a moment when a decision is made to let other people off the hook for what they did to you. It is a new way of living, an active, ongoing process of looking at your family and everyone around you through different eyes. When "other forgiveness" is present, it is apparent in every reaction to day-to-day living.

When you are conscious of the impact this disease has on the lives of everyone coming in contact with it, and have faced and released your emotional pain from the past, it is no longer difficult to be forgiving and compassionate toward others. There is less fear of being hurt again since you feel more control over whether or not you will allow that to happen in your life. There is no need to use anger or bitterness to protect yourself from pain. You are able to let go and love freely. The more connected you feel with your concept of your Higher Power, the easier this step becomes since the ultimate judgment of human behavior is not in our hands anyway.

As painful memories return, you do not need to find a scapegoat to blame for what happened. You feel the healing taking place and may not always need to share this right away with others. Sometimes the best thing to do is just cry. Occasional pain is part of everyone's life, not something to be avoided and blamed on others.

When we are living "other forgiveness" we are no longer victims, passively coping with whatever life hands us. We can be responsible for the outcome. Sometimes we would rather not be as informed as we become at this stage. Many recovering people have moments when they say "Oh, for the good old days when I could blame someone else!" But the good news is we can change just about anything in our own lives with help.

Working on bringing health into our relationships with our children and our family of origin can be a significant contribution to the future of our world. In "other forgiveness" we feel a responsibility to break the illness cycle by spreading our health around.

Our view of the world in general may change as we stop dividing the world into those who understand and are enlightened about this disease and those who don't.

I was recently asked at a public presentation "Why don't they understand and treat Adult Children properly?" (The person was referring to other professionals: doctors, etc.) My response was: "Why don't we build bridges and stop blaming them for what we haven't shared with them?" Blaming society is no more necessary than blaming our family.

We can develop an open forgiving attitude toward those who have not had these experiences, taking opportunities to educate, but more importantly, looking for what we can learn from the world. We do not have all the answers, and being an Adult Child or Grandchild or Recovering Alcoholic does not make us any less human. Finding the commonalities and joining the world in its struggle is what health is about.

SUMMARY

Although no two individuals will experience recovery in the same order or time-frame, the following guideposts are often part of the long term process.

Recovery Stages

STAGE I — What's Wrong With Me?

This stage is a beginning one, which might include the tasks of —
1. Identification of the problem
2. Breaking the "No Talk Rule"
3. Asking for help

STAGE II — Who Am I?

When giving up the pseudo or false identity, it is necessary to find out who we really are. Tasks include —
1. Learning self-caring as a way of life
2. Feeling the pain and sharing it as it occurs
3. Feel the fear and guilt and DO IT ANYWAY

STAGE III — Who Do I Want To Be?

Major changes are possible when the recovering person feels free to choose new beliefs, behaviors and attitudes. Tasks include:
1. Viewing recovery as an adventure rather than a goal.
2. Self-forgiveness
3. Other forgiveness

This process evolves to a point where it is no longer appropriately termed *RECOVERY* but more fittingly called *LIFE!*

_____Chapter 7_____

Changing Family Patterns

History is a powerful force, regardless of our efforts to overcome the negative aspects. Its influence in our present day interactions can be minimized, but accomplishing this takes great effort and a willingness to learn from scratch what other adults may take for granted.

Part of the responsibility that comes with recovery is to attempt to break the cycle of co-dependent patterns and abuse within a family system. This does not mean that every recovering person needs to try to change the people around him/her. It does mean that through modeling our own health and relating to those we love in a healthier manner, we can impact a family system. This does not require any conscious effort to change another person. Instead we find that as illness spreads, so may health. People are attracted to it, and may begin to change without even admitting they needed to.

It is never too late to begin. Whether children are toddlers, teens or grown adults, we can begin to model healthy adulthood, communication, intimacy, maturity, etc. The way we relate to our parents in recovery can also impact their behavior toward us and demonstrate to our children healthier ways of communicating. Both the previous generation — our parents — and the next generation — our children — have the potential for change, and one person's shift in attitude and behavior can make a significant difference.

As GCoAs and ACoAs learn about the damage in their families of origin, they are faced with the dilemma of knowing with certainty that they want it to be different for their children but, like their parents, have limited training and skill in the fine art of parenting. Grandchildren may have a slim advantage in this area if their parents had some success in creating the external appearance of healthy family. This too can be deceiving and lead the GCoA to believe they know how to do it, when the reality is they know little about intimacy, honest communication and unconditional love.

It is unrealistic to expect to eliminate co-dependency entirely from a family system. It is with us to stay, but each generation can contribute to adding healthier behaviors, which will minimize the negative consequences for the next. Incorporating new found health into present relationships without alienating, preaching or intimidating those we love is not an easy task. It is important to remember that they have the right to stay the same if they choose. We do not have the power or the authority to decide who needs to get well and how. We can only live as healthy individuals, hoping that as they see us flourish, others may choose to join us. While the children are young, we have greater influence and opportunity to guide them into healthier patterns of behavior.

Dealing With Your Children

When I share this information with professionals and recovering people, I am confronted with a barrage of questions, particularly from the parents in the group about how this is done. The following are the most common concerns expressed, along with some suggestions:

1. I want my children to be able to express feelings, but how much anger should I allow?

Many ACoA/GCoAs have never witnessed healthy expression of anger and are fearful that they, or their children, will lose control if it is openly expressed. Others believe that since they weren't allowed to do it, their children should have total freedom of expression. Both views reflect the extreme thinking of co-dependency.

When we have had no experience with something, it is always a good idea to look for people who have had and watch them. Most of us can find a family where children are given limits but are still able to be angry on occasion. Talking to others and drawing from their experience can prevent us from having to learn everything the hard way.

Once again the example we set as adults is probably the most important parenting tool we have. What you *do* when you are angry with your spouse, friend or child is what will be imitated by your children. What you *say* about healthy expression of anger has a very minor influence.

During our daily interaction with our children, it is natural for differences of opinion to occur. When a child is asked to clean up the kitchen, the reaction is unlikely to be positive. Anger in the form of irritation, frustration, annoyance is an everyday event in almost every family.

Rage as a reaction to this type of situation is not a normal response and is an indicator that professional help is needed. Rageful reactions may include violent outbursts, verbal abuse, destruction of property over minor issues.

In response to "normal" anger, a parent may set some limits on the amount of disagreement to permit, e.g., how long you will discuss the issue, how loud a child can be, will name-calling be permitted, is "I hate you!" an acceptable thing to say and what about door slamming? The important thing is that the parent has decided in advance what is permissible and what will happen when the limit is crossed.

For instance, "I will listen to your side as long as you are within reason, but if not, you must go to your room for 10 minutes and come back when you calm down."

Parents also lose control of tempers at times and may also need "time out". Hopefully you will be able to see it coming and limit yourself.

Healthy expression of anger should never include physical contact, destruction of property or verbal abuse which detracts from self-esteem. When these things happen, and they do in all families at some time or another, there are consequences. It is usually a good idea to take some time to think about consequences, rather than imposing them in the middle of an argument.

If your marriage or other significant relationships with adults includes this type of destructive expression of anger, your parenting will be ineffective until this is addressed. Remember — Your children are watching you!

2. How much emotion should I show around my children when I'm feeling bad myself?

During active addiction or similar family stress, many ACoA/GCoAs witnessed parents weeping, screaming, being extremely fearful or depressed, without regard for the impact this may have had on them as children. In reaction, the recovering person may believe that children should never see parents hurting. This may be particularly true for GCoAs whose parents were trying hard to "do it right" and showed no emotion in the process.

Children need to see their parents as real people with feelings in order to learn how to be "real people with feelings" when they grow up. There is a difference between letting them see feelings, and imposing our feelings on our children with the expectation that they will make us feel better.

I believe it is acceptable to let a child see an adult looking sad, as long as the child is reassured that they are not responsible for it and that the adult is doing something to take care of him/herself. Excessive tears, or open detailed discussion of the problem in front of a child (of any age) can leave the child fearing abandonment. Talking on the telephone to friends about your pain, while children are close by, may be very destructive, even though it is done unconsciously.

Children should not be asked to understand or support parents through hard times. They may be asked to be patient and tolerant with a parent for a short time until the crisis is over. This presents a healthy message to a child of "I have needs, too." If the "hard time" extends into months or longer, it may be necessary to bring other people into the child's life (professionals, family or friends) who can be fun, while supporting the child until you are more available.

It is amazing how quickly our children, even if very young, begin protecting us when we are hurting. Don't be afraid to bring up the subject around them — they are probably not discussing it because they are afraid it will upset you, not the other way around.

For example, "I'm feeling sad today, missing your Dad, but it seems to be getting easier. How about you?"

When we hurt, our children hurt. Sharing it openly without depending on them can make the process move along more quickly for all concerned.

3. *What if my spouse won't cooperate with my attempts to be a better parent? I feel like I'm doing it alone.*

My research with Grandchildren and experience with ACoAs tells me consistently that every little bit helps. Having one healthy parent is better than having none. Somehow children are able to sort out the healthy from the unhealthy and make their own choices as they get older. It is very important, however, that you do not get into the "good guy" versus "bad guy" game. Even the unwilling partner has some good things to offer, and there is no such thing as a *right way*.

As the enlightened parent you do have a responsibility to protect your children from serious harm. This may require you to take a hard look at your marriage, particularly if you or your children are being abused. Sometimes the only way to stop the abuse is to get out.

Assuming this is not the case, uneven parenting is a difficult but not impossible situation. It may help to try to come to some agreement about types of discipline you will or will not be using in your family. For example, you may at least be able to agree not to use physical punishment or to verbally abuse children into compliance. You may agree that threats of throwing a child out of the house, or other harmful and unrealistic comments, be eliminated. Be very clear about what you are willing to accept. You may try suggesting parenting classes, or good books to read, but if resistance is there, these measures will probably not help. Get help yourself, and maybe your health will rub off a little in time.

Being honest with your children about your differences will prevent some of the manipulation that results from uneven parenting.

"I know your Dad would do it differently, but this is between you and I and you will have to live with my limits this time."

Children want limits and eventually will prefer the healthier method of parenting because it is more consistent, respectful and predictable. They will always know where you stand.

The bad news is the older the children, the more difficult the transition. Adolescents who have lived within a dysfunctional family system and to some degree ineffective parenting, may choose the old way rather than change. This is hard for a recovering parent to accept.

Acceptance does not mean resignation to a family with abuse and no limits. Limits can be set and enforced but expect resistance and be willing to let go of the little things. Save your energy for what is really essential and important to you. Get professional advice as you go through it. When all else fails, rest assured they will grow up and may even understand at the age of 19 that you were only trying to help.

One final suggestion: take a look at your marriage. Could it be that the disagreements around parenting are a "smoke screen" for bigger issues? Be aware of the example this is setting for your children regarding intimate relationships, problem-solving, shared responsibility, etc.

4. What is the difference between healthy discipline and abuse?

The harsh discipline in abusive families leads to low self-esteem in children. It is an attempt on the part of parents, who are feeling inadequate, to control behavior through fear, guilt and conditional love. It teaches very little about self-discipline or healthy choicemaking and may gain compliance, but for all the wrong reasons.

Effective parenting does not put the parent/child relationship on the line with every disagreement.

"I don't love you anymore because you disappointed me. You are worthless . . ."

Discipline is most effective when it allows the natural consequences in any situation to "teach the lesson". A child who continuously refuses to get up in the morning is given an alarm clock and expected to wake himself. If the school bus is missed, he/she walks to school (if possible) or must pay for a cab, etc. No anger on the part of the parent is necessary.

Whenever possible, it works best to let our children learn from their own actions and choices. Granted, solutions are not always this simple but abuse is not necessary to control behavior in any situation.

I am often asked questions like, "What if my teenager refuses to do what I say? Nothing works. If I ground her, she just goes out the window anyway." This chapter is not intended to address damage of this extent. Professional intervention is necessary when a situation is this out of control.

Among the references at the end of the book are a few excellent resources on parenting which teach you to think more creatively about natural consequences while concentrating on raising self-esteem in your children.

5. What is the difference between praise and affirmation?

Grandchildren of Alcoholics are often very confused by the fact that they heard many positive comments growing up, but have low self-worth as adults. This could be because what they received was praise for doing good things, without any consistent affirmation for just being. Their ACoA parent may have tried to convey approval and encouragement by noticing and commenting on each and every good thing the child did, but neglected to say "I love you when you don't do anything, too!"

The ideal is not a matter of either praise or affirmation exclusively, but a healthy balance of both. Praise is a positive statement to another person that their behavior meets with our approval. It feels good to be the receiver of the praise, but in order to feel good again, they must do something else that meets with our approval.

Affirmations might sound more like "I'm glad you are here. I love you just the way you are." It is not necessarily attached to any behavior and has little to do with approval. It means that I accept you as you are and I want you to feel good about yourself. The approval of a parent is not as important as the approval of oneself.

Some children are better at accomplishing praise-worthy things than others. The "family hero" type often thrives on the attention and praise elicited by his/her achievements. Ironically, although they may receive more praise and approval than the other children in the family, their self-esteem is no better. It creates a vicious cycle of try harder, do more and do it better than everyone else. The child receives the message that he must earn love and is not taught to evaluate his own actions and to give himself strokes.

Examples of Affirmations:

> I'm glad you're a boy/girl.
> It's nice that you have such strong ideas about what you want.
> It's okay to make mistakes.
> All your feelings are okay with me.
> You can trust your own instincts.
> You don't have to do tricks to please me.

Adults in recovery find it a difficult task to even think of affirmations since most were raised with criticism. We need to give the same affirmations to ourselves that we are giving to our children. It may look funny at first, but posting some around the house can help to remind you of how special you are, too.

6. What is healthy detachment from children?

The concept of detachment, reinforced through the Al-Anon program, is intended to help each of us to be responsible for our own feelings. It teaches that we cannot control or accept responsibility for the actions of others, especially an active alcoholic, and that letting go with love will actually aid in creating an environment for the other person to change themselves. It does not mean angry and resentful resignation at our inability to fix another person. It also does not mean a shirking of our responsibility as a parent.

When dealing with a difficult child or teenager, it is very tempting to write them off, throw up our hands and say, "I'll just detach, because nothing else works!"

I'm reminded of a mother who called me to report her "progress" since treatment and Al-Anon. She stated, "I'm going to meetings and letting go of control. I just don't get upset the way I used to. My 13-year-old daughter is into drugs and shoplifting. I've done everything I could do and she just won't listen, so now it's time to *detach*. If she wants to live that way, that's her business."

Although it is possible to detach emotionally so that we are not personally destroyed by our children's mistakes, our job is not over just because we don't know what to do next. It just means we are going to have to use professionals and our support system to survive the crisis. While we detach emotionally from the anger and acting out, the job of setting limits and natural consequences while affirming the person will continue.

Healthy detachment from a child begins with the "terrific twos". We learn as parents not to take personally a child's statement of independence. It is sometimes necessary to protect them from themselves until they have developed the skill to handle new tasks. Having confidence in ourselves as parents (saying often to yourself and your child "I am the grown-up Mom/Dad. You are the child. I know what I'm doing, even when you don't understand it") will help you to let go and know you are doing a good job.

It helps a great deal to read about child development, talk to other parents with the same age children, ask your family doctor or a therapist what you can expect of a child this age. Detachment from children is not the same as detachment from adults. We cannot let go completely until our job is done. There is no magical age at which this happens, and it is different in every case. It is also not an event, but a gradual process of letting the young person use independently what you have taught, and handle the consequences of their own choices.

7. What do we do about drugs and alcohol when we know our children are at high risk?

Many recovering adult have out of fear, fallen into using the *3 Ps:* Prevention through Preaching and Paranoia! They are sure their children are going to be addicted. They can tell by their "alcoholic personalities" as infants. They talk about alcoholism daily and give lectures from age five on about "What it did to me." The first time their child experiments with drugs or alcohol they cart him down to the drunk tank at the police station or the local detox and insist that he be evaluated and go to open AA meetings for a month.

Once again parents must remember that the modeling they provide for their children is the most important factor in how they are going to turn out. We cannot eliminate the physiological predisposition in our families. We will probably be unsuccessful in convincing our children that they should never try drugs or alcohol because of being at risk. Society has a powerful influence.

The "teetotaling" families, by the way, produce a lot of alcoholism, too.

We are left with trying to be good parents in every area so that drugs and alcohol are not the "only way out" for our children. Many young people initially try to get self-esteem from a chemical because they have not received it at home. Addiction then blossoms in a fertile environment.

The simple statement "Just Say No!" is one that many children of alcoholics may not be able to make. If our parenting teaches healthy choicemaking in all areas, we will not have to make a major issue of this one. If abuse or addiction does happen, our children will probably reach out for help much earlier because of our example. They know there is help. They know it is okay to ask for it. They know it's a disease that is treatable. They will not condemn themselves and suffer from the shame and stigma that their parents or grandparents did. They will not be as damaged as you were.

Recovering parents in particular may have exaggerated fears, expecting that their children will have to go down the same road they did. If you are an effective parent in other areas and model the behavior of a healthy, growing adult, it is unlikely that your children will ever see the road you were on, even if they become addicted.

8. Should I force my children into treatment for co-dependency if they don't want it?

The answer to this question depends a great deal on the age of the child, although the numerical age is not always the best indicator. Somewhere around age 12 to 14 parents can no longer insist that their children blindly follow their direction. They need at that time to have more input into decisions, and if they strongly disapprove, chances are they will sabotage anything they are forced to do.

Not every child must get treatment for co-dependency, but I believe each should have an opportunity if it is available. One very effective way to get children, even resistant ones, into treatment is to work out a family treatment plan with a professional. This means that every one in the family is going to do something toward their own and the family's recovery. The plan may even be written and signed by each family member. The role of parents in the plan is to convey the message that we are all willing to do what is necessary to repair what damage has been done. This may also mean that some family members need more treatment than others.

In my experience with children and adolescents in a short-term residential program, every child has some resistance. This does not mean they won't respond to treatment. Some teenagers, especially scapegoats, may desperately want treatment but be unwilling to admit it openly. However, if a child is adamant about not going for counseling, I would not insist, but continue with the family treatment plan, offering help again at another time.

Treatment has been used as an "or else" in some cases. For instance, a runaway teen cannot come home unless she agrees to get treatment. With young people who are extremely resistant, we need to take advantage of these special "opportunities" to offer help.

Additional Suggestions For Bringing Recovery Into The Family

• **Adequate family time** — Don't let 12-step meetings prevent quality family time. Children will only appreciate the program if it enhances their lives. Once the initial recovery period is passed, balance your meetings, time with spouse, time alone and family time.

• **Expect stress and prepare for it when possible** — Instead of living from crisis to crisis, whether it is financial, health, housecleaning, car repairs, etc., look ahead and prevent what you can. This will bring more stability to your home and teach children about the "real world". Whenever it feels like everything is totally out of control, reverting to some established routine may help, e.g., a set dinner time, homework time, family TV time. Even sticking to this order for one week can restore sanity to a seemingly crazy situation.

• **Family meetings** — Many families benefit from an established get-together each week, where anything can be discussed from family vacation plans to balancing chores. The important thing is that everyone gets a chance to talk and listen. By the way, children will tell you they hate these meetings. Don't believe it! They miss them when they don't have them.

• **Use the "I'll think about it" technique** — This is a useful tool in any setting, but especially at home. Even when you are fairly sure of your response to a request, take a little time and don't give an answer just because the pressure is on. On really tough decisions, it may be necessary to get input from several sources: spouse, therapist, sponsor, etc., followed by some quiet soul-searching of your own. I often advise, "Go off in a closet and ask yourself what you want to do." Children will respect a well thought-out decision more than an angry or impulsive reaction, even when it isn't in their favor.

• **Get clear with yourself and your spouse on who is in charge** — As parents you are boss but just saying it isn't enough; you need to believe it. Parents need to be in a strong partnership where communication is open and frequent. Disagreements will occur but do not need to be resolved in the presence of children. It's okay to let them know you are struggling with something, but don't put them in the middle of it.

Children need to see and hear that your job is to guide and protect them, even when they don't like it, and that you take your job very seriously.

• **Work on Family Defensiveness** — Once families have begun treatment there is no need for strong protection from one another. The old "What do you mean by that?" can be replaced with "I'm trying to understand you, will you explain that again?"

Old habits die slowly and the spontaneous defensive reactions can gradually be replaced with trust and openness.

• **Remain open to change.** — ACoA/GCoAs have been allowing history to determine how they will relate to those they love, doing either the same thing their parents did, or the direct opposite. Children may have some good ideas about how to change a family for the better. Be willing to read, discuss, study, take courses and get professional help periodically to get through the rough spots and learn new ways of relating.

A Word about Dealing with Grown Children:

For some of you reading this book, it may be a bit late to dramatically change your family situation since your children are grown. Many of these concepts still apply but it is important to respect your children's rights to learn for themselves. You may want to get into recovery and see the light now, but your example may be the only thing that makes a difference.

Remember also that they don't have to do it the same way you did. Grandchildren and Great-Grandchildren may not understand the need to label the problem as co-dependency. Any good counseling and support system can make a difference. Rather than preaching or alienating, *show* them what a recovering person looks like, and that it is never too late to start.

Dealing With Your Parents

For some Grandchildren and ACoAs in recovery the good news is the bad news. They struggle between "Isn't it wonderful that I've found out what's wrong with me" and "I'm afraid to let my parents in on the wonderful news that I'm recovering from what they couldn't give me." The exceeding loyalty felt toward their family of origin leads the ACoA/GCoA to hide their co-dependent recovery from their family and regress to a "little girl/boy" state when in the presence of parents.

Once an individual is in the process of recovery and the beginnings of the forgiveness stage, incorporating new skills in relating to parents and family can also begin.

Here are a few guidelines which may be helpful:

• **Accept your parents and family "AS IS".** Stop trying to change them, even indirectly through subtle suggestions. Try not to evaluate their actions and judge the quality of their lives. Al-Anon can help a great deal with this.

• **Take an inventory of the "good things" you received from your parents.** If nothing else, you may have inherited a few talents through genetics. Acknowledge these. Once you have genuinely dealt with the pain of the past, this should not be difficult to do. If it is, you may not be finished with your anger yet. You may want to keep this positive list handy for the times when you question whether there was anything good in your childhood.

• **Avoid family gossip and indirect communication.** What you don't know won't hurt you. Carrying messages or keeping secrets for siblings will contribute to your own negativity. Conversations or "bitch sessions" about Mom or Dad will not ease family tension or in any way contribute to progress in healthier relating. Sometimes siblings really have nothing else to say. You may need to find new subjects to talk about, or simply talk less often.

• **Do what feels good to you, rather than following tradition or family expectation.** Just ask yourself "Do I want to be there for dinner?" You may find that you really do want to be there but your attitude will be better if you've made a conscious choice. Learn about your own time limits. You know when you've had enough family time and need to get out. Preparing in advance for a smooth exit at about that time can prevent hard feelings. Always have a plan which keeps you feeling in charge of your own behavior. Getting caught up in the plans of others leaves you feeling angry and helpless. You can always choose to go along, but having an alternate plan in mind will help.

• **Refuse to be in the presence of abuse by your parents to each other or anyone else.** Especially don't allow them to abuse you. When it starts, whether on the telephone or at a family gathering, quietly remove yourself from the situation. No anger is necessary, just take care of yourself. When things calm down, you may try to express your feelings about it as honestly as possible.

• **Consider the consequences before becoming vulnerable around parents** who are abusive, manipulative or unresponsive to your needs. Ask yourself if it is really worth the price you pay to open up emotionally to your parents. You may choose to stick to safer topics and save the vulnerable feelings for your support system.

• **Rather than forcing communication and intimacy, take advantage of the special moments that occur naturally.** In every family there will be times when a parent or sibling is ready to open up more than usual. Maybe they are hurting or especially happy and want to share that with you. Or perhaps they are momentarily curious about your recovery. This is the time to share more openly than usual. It may not happen again for a long time, so enjoy and appreciate this brief connection.

• **Do not become the family expert on alcoholism.** This one is difficult to avoid even outside of the family. When the subject comes up, you don't have to comment, correct mistaken information, teach, preach or refer for treatment. People who really don't want help will set you up for these discussions, and you may have to walk away enraged while they are unaffected. You may offer a phone number for them to call if they are serious, but don't try to be the one with the answers. It's okay to say "I don't know," even when you do.

• **If your parents are in an active addiction you may need to consult a professional,** trained in intervention techniques, to evaluate that possibility. It is much easier to let go when you truly believe you have done all there is to do. Intervention is not always appropriate, especially if it has been attempted before or the person has already had extensive treatment. When appropriate, it not only accomplishes the impossible in many cases — getting the addict to treatment — but it begins a healing process within a family system.

• **The dramatic changes _you_ make in recovery may be most apparent outside of your family.** The last place you will begin to show your health is in your relationships with your parents. This is not always bad since they need time to adjust to the new you. It is not necessary to immediately expose your new assertiveness or honesty and expect them to rejoice in the positive changes you've made. Show your real self to them gradually. They will probably see you as a little "strange" at first but will come to accept the changes in time if they are not too intimidated.

SUMMARY

No one can recover in a vacuum and the significant relationships in the lives of the ACoA/GCoA are immediately impacted by even positive changes. A major responsibility in recovery is to do what one can to break the cycle of co-dependency and addiction in the family system, particularly the next generation.

There is a great deal to learn about effective parenting. Using every possible resource is a good idea when you don't have the modeling of your own parents to draw from.

Some of the areas to be addressed in the home are . . .

• Teaching children to express anger appropriately

- Expressing your feelings without burdening children
- Uneven parenting — "Doing it alone", if necessary
- Practicing healthy discipline and natural consequences
- Affirming children and yourself
- Learning healthy detachment from children's anger
- Handling the issue of drugs and alcohol with children
- Encouraging children to get treatment for co-dependency

Coping with your own parents while making dramatic changes in your own life can be a major challenge. Slowly exposing your family to the new you is more likely to be successful.

Some additional suggestions to ease the transition:

- Inventory the good things they gave you — even genetic
- Avoid family gossip and indirect communication
- Do what feels good to you regarding family events
- Refuse to be around abuse or to be abused by parents
- Think before "opening up" your vulnerabilities to them
- Don't force communication; look for opportunities
- Don't become the family expert on alcoholism
- Intervene if parents are in active addiction
- Give parents time to get used to the new you

References And Suggested Reading

Ackerman, Robert, **Children of Alcoholics,** Holmes Beach, Florida: Learning Publications, Inc., 1983.

Black, Claudia, **It Will Never Happen To Me,** Denver, Colorado: M.A.C., Printing and Publications Div., 1982.

Diaz, P. and O'Gorman, P., **Breaking The Cycle of Addiction,** Pompano Beach, Florida: Health Communications, 1987.

Dreikurs, Rudolph M.D., **Children The Challenge,** New York: Hawthorn/Dutton, 1964.

Illsley-Clarke, Jeanne, **Self-Esteem: A Family Affair,** Plymouth MN. JI Consultants, 1980.

Satir, Virginia, **Conjoint Family Therapy,** Palo Alto, California: Science and Behavior Books, Inc., 1967.

Smith, Ann W., "Treatment Issues for Addicted Children from Alcoholic Families", *Focus on Family and Chemical Dependency, U.S. Journal of Drug and Alcohol Dependence,* March/April, 1985.

Wegscheider-Cruse, Sharon, **Another Chance**, Palo Alto, California: Science and Behavior Books, 1981.

Woititz, Janet, **Adult Children of Alcoholics**, Pompano Beach, Florida: Health Communications, Inc., 1983.